PATHS

*A collection of essays on different
techniques of Meditation according to
different faiths.*

Sri Ramakrishna Math

MYLAPORE MADRAS 600 004

Published by
Adhyaksha
Sri Ramakrishna Math
Mylapore, Chennai-4

**Total number of copies
printed before: 35,600**

XIII-2M 3C-10-2013
ISBN 81-7120-144-X

Printed in India at
Sri Ramakrishna Math Printing Press
Mylapore, Chennai-4

CONTENTS

iv

PUBLISHER'S NOTE

We have great pleasure in placing before our readers this short symposium on Paths of Meditation.

Originally contributed as articles for the 1979 Special Number of the *Vedanta Kesari,* these essays present an interesting cross section of the diverse theories and techniques relating to the art and science of Meditation. The writers are not only specialists, each in his own field, but speak from deep personal experience. They write, therefore, not like scribes but with authority.

Meditation is not escapism. It is neither an imposition nor a luxury. It is as indispensable for the spiritual life as breathing is for the physical. To meditate is to open the door of the mind to the spaciousness that is our birthright. Devoid of meditation, one is like a blind man in a world of light and colour and loveliness. Our prayer is that ·this handy volume may serve as an eye-opener to all seekers of the supreme fulfilment.

Sri Ramakrishna Math, Madras.
Kalpataru Day,
1-1-1980   Publisher

MEDITATION ACCORDING
TO THE TRINITY

IN THE WORDS OF
SRI RAMAKRISHNA

If a man is able to weep for God, he will
see Him. He will go into Samadhi. Perfection
in yoga is Samadhi. A man achieves Kumbhaka without any Yogic exercise if he but weeps
for God. The next stage is Samadhi.

There is another method — that of meditation. In the Sahasrara, Siva manifests himself in a special manner. The aspirant should
meditate on Him. The body is like a tray ;
the mind and Buddhi are like water. The
Sun of Satchidananda is reflected in this water.
Meditating on the reflected sun one sees the
Real Sun through the grace of God.

The first stage is that of the beginner. He
studies and hears. Second is the stage of the
struggling aspirant. He prays to God, meditates on Him and sings His names and glories.
The third stage is is that of the perfect

soul. He has seen God, realized Him directly
and immediately in his inner consciousness.
Last is the stage of the supremely perfect, like
Chaitanya. Such a devotee establishes a definite relationship with God, looking on Him as
his Son or Beloved.

The heart is a splendid place. One can
meditate there or in the Sahasrara. There
are rules for meditation given in the scriptures.
But you may meditate wherever you like. Every
place is filled with Brahman-Consciousness.
Is there any place where It does not exist ?
Narayana in Bali's presence covered with two
steps the heavens, the earth and the interspaces.
Is there any place left uncovered by God ? A
dirty place is as holy as the bank of the Ganges.
It is said that the whole creation is the Virat,
the Universal Form of God.

There are two kinds of meditation, one on
the formless God and the other on God with
form. But meditation on the formless God is
extremely difficult. In that meditation you
must wipe out all that you see or hear. You
contemplate only on the nature of your inner
self. Meditating on His inner self Siva dances
about. He exclaims, "What am I ? What
am I ? " This is called the Siva Yoga. While

practising this form of meditation one directs one's look to the forehead. It is meditation on the nature of one's inner self after negating the world, following the Vedantic method of Neti, Neti.

There is another form of meditation known as the Vishnu Yoga. The eyes are fixed on the tip of the nose. Half the look is directed inward, and the other half outward. This is how one meditates on God with form. Sometimes Siva meditates on God with form, and dances. At that time he exclaims 'Rama, Rama' and dances about. God is born as man for the purpose of sporting as man. Rama, Krishna and Chaitanya are examples. By meditating on an Incaranation of God one meditates on God Himself.

When I meditated during my Sadhana, I used to think of the unflickering flame of a lamp set in a windless place.

In deep meditation a man is not at all conscious of the outer world.

A person can achieve such single-mindedness in meditation that he will see nothing, hear nothing. He will not be conscious even of touch. A snake may crawl over his body but he will not know it. Neither of them will be aware of the other.

In deep meditation the sense organs stop functioning, the mind does not look outward. It is like closing the gate of the outer court in a house. There are five objects of the senses ; form, taste, smell, touch and sound. They are all left outside.

At the beginning of meditation the objects of the senses appear before the aspirant. But when the meditation becomes deep they no longer bother him. They are left outside. How many things I saw during meditation ! I vividly perceived before me a heap of rupees, a shawl, a plate of sweets and two women with rings in their noses. ' What do you want ? ' I asked my mind. ' Do you want to enjoy any of these things ? ' ' No ', replied the mind, ' I don't want any of them. I don't want anything but the Lotus Feet of God .'

Nangta used to tell me how a Jnani meditates. Everywhere is water ; all the regions above and below are filled with water ; man, like a fish, is swimming joyously in that water. In real meditation you will actually see all this.

Do you know another way a Jnani meditates ? Think of infinite Akasa, and a bird flying there, joyously spreading its wings. There is the Chidakasa, and Atman is the bird. The bird is not imprisoned in a cage ; it flies in the Chidakasa. Its joy is limitless.

Do you know what one feels in meditation ? The mind becomes like a continuous flow of oil — it thinks of one object only, and that is God. It does not think of anything else.

IN THE WORDS OF
THE HOLY MOTHER

Meditate and pray to the particular aspect of the Divinity revealed to you. The meditation begins in the heart and ends in the head. Neither Mantra nor scripture is of any avail. Bhakti or devotion alone accomplishes everything.

Continuous meditation will make the mind so steady that you will not feel inclined to give it up. When the mind is not in a mood to meditate, do not force it to do so. In such conditions, get up from the seat of meditation after making prostrations. Real meditation is of a spontaneous nature.

If meditation is not possible do Japa. Realization will come through Japa. If the meditative mood comes, well and good ; but by no means do it by force.

One must practise meditation and Japa. That removes the impurities of the mind.

As one gets the fragrance of a flower by handling it, as one gets the smell of sandalwood by rubbing it against a stone, in the same way one gets spiritual awakening by constantly thinking of God. Sit for meditation in the morning and evening. Keep your head cool and practise meditation and prayer. It is very difficult to do so. It is rather easy to dig the earth with a spade.

IN THE WORDS OF SWAMI VIVEKANANDA

When the mind has been trained to remain fixed on a certain internal or external location, there comes to it the power of flowing in an unbroken current, as it were, towards that point. This state is called Dhyana.

The meditative state is the highest state of existence.

When by the previous preparations, it becomes strong and controlled and has the power of finer perception, the mind should be employed in meditation. This meditation must begin with gross objects and slowly rise to finer and finer, until it becomes objectless.

When one's Self is meditated upon as zero, and bereft of quality, that is called Abhava. That in which one sees the Self as full of bliss and bereft of all impurities, and one with God is called Mahayoga. The Yogi, by each method, realizes the self.

The multiplicity of waves gives place to unity and one wave is left in the mind. This is Dhyana, meditation.

Whenever the Yogi meditates, he can keep out all other thoughts ; he becomes identified with that on which he meditates. When he meditates, he is like a piece of crystal. Before flowers the crystal becomes almost identified with the flowers. If the flower is red, the crystal looks red, or if the flower is blue the crystal looks blue.

Dharana is holding the mind on to some particular object. An unbroken flow of knowledge in that object is Dhyana.

If the mind can be fixed on the centre for twelve seconds it will be a Dharana, twelve such Dharnas will be a Dhyana, and twelve such Dhyanas will be a Samadhi.

With every sense and every organ active, have you that tremendous peace so that nothing can disturb you ? Standing in Market Street waiting for the car with all the rush going on around you, are you in meditation — calm and peaceful ? In the cave are you intensely active there with all quiet about you ? If you are, you are a Yogi; otherwise not.

Take some holy person, some great person whom you revere, some saint whom you know to be perfectly non-attached, and think of his heart. That heart has become non-attached, and meditate on that heart ; it will calm the mind.

Meditation is the removal of attachment ; it is perfected by the suppression of the modifications. Also by non-attachment and practice, meditation is perfected.

The greatest help to spiritual life is meditation (Dhyana). In meditation we divest ourselves of all material conditions and feel our divine nature. We do not depend upon any external help in meditation.

Meditation is a constant remembrance (of the thing meditated upon) flowing like an unbroken stream of oil poured from one vessel to another.

When the Jiva is sought to be united with Brahman, it is best ; when meditation is practised, it is medium ; repetition of name is the lowest form, and external worship is the lowest of the low. You must try to combine in your life immense idealism with immense practicality. You must be prepared to go into deep meditation now, and the next moment you must be ready to go and cultivate those fields.

After initiation there should be in the aspirant after truth, Abhyasa or repeated attempt at practical application of the Truth by prescribed means of constant meditation upon the chosen ideal.

Meditation is the one thing. Meditate, the greatest thing is meditation. It is the nearest approach to spiritual life — the mind meditating. It is the one moment in our daily life when we are not at all material — the soul thinking of itself, free from all matter, this marvellous touch of the soul.

Meditation is the focussing of the mind on some object. If the mind acquires concentration on one object, it can be so concentrated on any object whatsoever.

First, the practice of meditation has to proceed with some one object before the mind. Once I used to concentrate my mind on some black point. Ultimately, during those days I could not see the point any more, or notice, that the point was before me at all — the mind used to be no more — no wave of functioning would rise, as if it were all an ocean without any breath of air. In that state I used to experience glimpses of superconscious truth. So I think, the practice of meditation even with some trifling external object leads to mental concentration. But it is true that the mind very easily attains calmness when one practises meditation with anything on which one's mind is most apt to settle down. This is the reason why we have in this country so much worship of the images of gods and goddesses. The fact however is that the objects of meditation can never be the same in the case of all men. People have proclaimed and preached to others only those external objects to which they held to become perfected in meditation. Oblivious of the fact, later on, that these objects are aids to the attainment of perfect mental calmness, men have extolled them beyond everything else. They have wholly concerned themselves with the means, getting comparatively unmindful of the end. The real aim is to make the mind functionless, but this cannot be done unless one becomes absorbed in some object.

When the meditation is deep one sees many wonderful things. While meditating at the Baranagore Math, one day I saw the nerves Ida and Pingala. One can see them with a little effort. Then when one has a vision of the Sushumna one can see anything one likes. If a man has unflinching devotion to the Guru, spiritual practices — meditation and Japam, etc., — come quite naturally ; we need not struggle for them. The Guru is Brahma, the Guru is Vishnu, and the Guru is Siva Himself.

As churning brings out the butter in the milk, so Dhyana brings the realization of Brahman in the Soul.

PROLOGUE

WHY MEDITATE

Meditation is a portmanteau word. It means many things to many men. A plethora of concepts get packed in that one elastic expression. Meditation spans an astonishingly broad spectrum of mental functions from the grossest scheming to the finest non-thinking. A Hitler meditates on the extermination of the entire Jewish race ; a politician meditates on ways and means of topping the polls and feathering his own nest ; a Gandhi meditates on the establishment of Rama Rajya and the settlement of all conflicts through non-violence; a Yogi meditates to gain perfect control over the turbulent senses ; and Siva meditates for no reason whatsoever ! What then is the focus of meditation ? What is its quintessence ?

The dictionary helps. We find in it the term 'meditation' derived from the Latin word 'MEDITARI' which means 'to heal'. Meditation is part of the science and art of healing.

To meditate is to set in motion processes that lead to the restoration of one's well-being — physical, mental, spiritual. We are only too painfully conscious what an incredible bundle of ailments and grievances each one of us is. Whatever facade we may manage to put up, inside it is all agony and frustration. *'Duḥkhā-layam, aśāśvatam'* says the Lord in the Gita, characterising this life of ours. The world we live in is sorrow's shrine. It echoes and re-echoes with the mocking laughter of transitoriness. The whole life is a ceaseless struggle to ward off misery and gain a bit of pleasure. As Swami Vivekananda has aptly put it, misery is like rheumatism — you exorcise it from one limb only to find it firmly ensconced in another. There seems to be a rigid law of Conservation of Misery. The sum total of human suffering appears to be constant. Remove sorrow from one field of life, presto! it greets you with another face in another field. Can this iron chain be broken? Can we have happiness untainted by misery? Is it possible to enjoy unqualified bliss? Meditation says, ' Yes '. It accepts the mighty challenge and promises to heal our wounds. It can assist us to overcome handicaps and grow into wholeness. With the file of meditation the iron chain of

suffering can be snapped asunder. We need not
remain pathetic little fragments of humanity;
if we take the trouble, we can through meditation blossom into joyous integrated beings.

In the last analysis happiness and sorrow
reside in the mind. It is the mind that is the
cause of man's bondage, it is the mind that
is the cause of his freedom. Using the mind
we have been able to achieve the vast wonders
that constitute modern civilization. But with
the same mind we suffer untold agonies of
hatred and war, want and fear. This mind
is an Alladin's lamp that can conjure into existence comforts and luxuries galore, but it can
also raise Frankensteinian monsters that make
life a nightmare. Meditation is the technique
for diverting the wayward destructive mind
into planned, constructive channels. It is the
moderator that converts the devastating atom
bomb into the creative atomic reactor. The
nuclear reaction that takes place in both the
devices is the same. But whereas the immense
energy generated by the atom bomb destroys
like a river in flood, the controlled release
of power in the atomic reactor is like a well
dammed river that helps us to irrigate land and
produce electricity. Meditation turns a curse

into a blessing. It is the alchemy that trans-
mutes the dross of everyday life into the gold
of unalloyed bliss. The master-key of meditation opens all the doors in the grand mansion
of the soul.

How then to meditate ? Meditation is at
once simple and difficult. It requires no special
equipment, it costs nothing. But you must
have a *mind* to meditate. The will produces
the way. There should be a tremendous urge,
an intense concern that the *summum bonum*
should be realised in this very life. There
can be no instalment plan in gaining the Infinite. Here and now, with no conditional
clauses in small print, we must have that for
which we have assumed this life. We must
attain the Ultimate without any dilly-dallying,
free from all reservations. Given that irre-
pressible eagerness, each one of us can soar
on the wings of meditation to realms of breath-
bereaving loveliness and power.

What are the methods to be adopted in
meditation ? Are there proven procedures
that can deliver the goods ? Fortunately,
yes. Sadhakas and savants, saints and seers
ancient and modern, of the East and of the
West, have elaborated different systems and

tested many techniques that bring fulfilment.
In fact there is no religion or philosophy of
the spirit that does not lay down its own series
of steps for meditating. Buddhism, for inst-
ance, is based on the supreme enlightenment
gained by the Buddha in meditation. The
Noble Eight-fold Path, which summarises
the Buddhist way of life, is climaxed by meditation 'in which alone perfection lies, and
through which alone can one with patient toil
unveil the inner world of Reality.' The various
schools of Buddhism have prescribed different
but precise steps for reaching the threshold of
Nirvana. Zen again is derived from the Sanskrit *dhyana*. Its steps lead to *satori* or living
experience. The Ashtanga Yoga of Patanjali
and the percepts of the Christian churches are
all systematised meditations. This volume
presents a representative cross-section of the
diverse paths of meditation laid down by
various schools of spiritual striving.

A distinction must, however, be drawn between prayer and meditation. Prayer is essentially a supplication to an external Being or
Power. It is a yearning of the heart for things
it lacks. It is importuning a Higher Potency
to fulfil our wants and desires. But meditation

has no element of begging in it. It is a reorientation of the mind for producing the knowledge by which all that is rightly needed is acquired. It is a purified mind calling upon the wisdom that dwells within. While prayer is addressed to an outside Power, meditation seeks conscious union with the Truth inside. Desire is the motive force for all action. But whereas in prayer the desire is self-centred, in meditation one 'attaches one's belt to the Power-house of the universe', as R.W. Trine puts it. The contemplative works, not for himself but *bahujanahitāya, bahujanasukhāya,* for the welfare of the many, for the happiness of all. In meditation the dew drop merges in the Shining Sea.

Likewise, there is a line of demarcation between concentration and meditation. By concentration we mean the preliminary exercises in one-pointedness of thought which must of necessity precede success in meditation. Before an instrument can be used it must be forged properly. The mind with which contemplation is achieved must first be trained to develop the power of converging all its energies at any required point. Not that concentration *per se* has any ethical or spiritual value. It is indeed a common requisite for progress in any field of art or science.   A ballerina has to go through many physical exercises to make her limbs sufficiently pliable.   The fencer repeats postures and motions till he acquires precision of aim. The mind likewise has to be disciplined by a series of exercises till it becomes a search-light that can be focussed wherever desired and can be switched on or off at will.   But the concentration thus attained is neutral.   Like any instrument it can be used for good purposes or bad.   With a knife a surgeon saves the life of a patient; with a knife you can also cut another's throat.   With fire we can warm ourselves, cook our food and produce articles of utility in the factory ; with the same fire we can also destroy our neighbour's house.   Concentration gives us power, it is up to us to put it to the highest use.   And the highest use of a concentrated mind is in meditation.

Concentration is only a process.   It is useful in daily life at all levels, but has no moral or spiritual significance.   Meditation, on the contrary, produces a state of consciousness in which the spiritual point of view alone counts. The techniques of concentration can be taught openly, they can be sold for money.   No more reverence need be attached to such information than, say, to instructions about physical culture. In meditation, however, the aspirant enters another world. It is a dimension in which there is a revolutionary transvaluation of values. Motives become of paramount importance and purity of character an essential postulate. It is forbidden not only to sell but even to use for personal ends the knowledge and power meditation brings. In meditation one treads on holy ground. One may speak of one's achievements in concentration with anyone else. But what one experiences in meditation has to be kept an utmost secret. It is caviare to the general. Our spiritual adventures are not to be worn on our sleeves for daws to peck at. This is why we find many of our scriptures adding a stern foot note : ' What I have taught you is the secret of secrets. It is not to be imparted to the faithless '. When we first read such vetoes we are apt to wonder why so much fuss is made about something that looks commonplace. The fact is that the commonplace look of spiritural experiences is highly deceptive. An atom is invisibly small but within it is packed energy that can wipe away a Hiroshima or Nagasaki. The power that meditation brings is divine in its intensity and so has to be handled with the greatest care andkeenest wisdom.Hence also the importance of meditating in loneliness. We are advised to meditate in the darkness of the night, not only because it ensures an undisturbing environment, but also in order that other people may not know of our meditating. Meditation should not be a public performance but a private pursuit. The more secret it is, the more sacred it proves.

A tree is known by its fruit and the touchstone of meditation is its effect on character. Meditation leads to a spiritual rebirth, a return to the child state in the sense of an honesty of thought and speech and a simple directness of action. With it goes an astounding width of vision and an unfathomable inner quietude. To realise the marvellous impact of meditation on the individual's personality we need go no farther than to Sri Ramakrishna whose whole half-century of sojourn on earth was an object lesson in the contemplative way. The least an earnest aspirant can do is to tread in the footsteps of that Child of the Divine Mother, in whose presence every one, man and woman, young and old, felt the upsurge of supernal joy.

MEDITATION ACCORDING
TO THE BHAGAVATA

By

SWAMI SIDDHINATHANANDA

Tasmāt sarvātmanā tāta
nigṛhāṇa mano dhiyā
Mayi āveśitayā yukta
etāvān yogasamgrahaḥ

[Bh. XI.23.61]

' Do thou restrain by all means thy fickle mind, my son, by thy superior intelligence set steady on Me. This is the sum and substance of all Yoga '. So spake the Lord to Uddhava.

Meditation means reflection, derived, according to the Chambers' Dictionary, from the Latin *meditari* probably cognate with the Latin root *mederi,* meaning to heal. So, meditation is the science of healing in its origin. Most ailments are mental and physical, and then there are the purely mental ones. Primarily the component that needs healing is the mind. So meditation is identical with Yoga

which is defined as the prevention of mental
modifications. Mental modifications are the
root cause of all misery and their eradication
is the science of Yoga. Arresting of the ripples
is only the negative aspect of the process;
the positive aspect is the reflection on the wit-
nessing Self which is ever present. Self awareness is the goal of Yoga and the means is meditation. Dhyana is the term used by the Yoga
system for meditation. Dhyana has various
degrees of intensity; they are called Dharana,
Dhyana, and Samadhi. Dharana is the process of placing the mind on the object of meditation to the exclusion of contrary thoughts.
When the mental flow becomes steady and
deep, it is Dhyana. When the object of meditation alone remains to the exclusion of all else,
it is Samadhi. Samadhi is the end and the
other two, the process.

In Dhyana or meditation, there are three
factors: the meditator, the process of meditation and the object of meditation. Of these
three, the first two are constant factors in any
form of meditation. The possibility of difference, if any, is only in the object. Here also,
there cannot be any real difference in the object
but, only in the conception of the object. When
one speaks of 'Meditation according to the

Bhagavata', the qualification on 'Meditation' can apply only to the object. For, in meditation, whether it be according to the *Bhagavata* or the Yoga Sutras, the person and the process are the same. The objects may differ. The Yoga Sutras suggest a few such as God, a flame, a saint and so on. The *Bhagavata* elaborates this to infinite proportions and at the same time provides a supreme, sublime person as the object of meditation.

Meditation is the soul of spiritual life. A life without meditation is like a horse without reins or a boat without rudder. That science has been perfected by Patanjali. All types of aspirants have adopted that method with suitable modifications to attain their goals. Mind is the object of attack for all. It is an internal instrument evolved by the soul out of subtle matter. Subtle matter by association with the luminous soul becomes live and serves both its father, the soul and its mother, Nature, *i.e.,* the body. Though it was intended to be a loyal servant of the soul, it played foul and started serving the demands of its material parent, with the result that the soul has been caught in interminable woes and worries. It is like the filament of an electric bulb claiming the luminosity to itself. Rightly has it been

compared to a drunk and maddened monkey.
It is this monkey thas has to be tackled. The
strange part of it is that the hero and the villain
are the same mind. The mind has to be trained
to conquer itself. It is almost an impossible
task and often, very exasperating. Arjuna
was perfectly right when he compared the
attempt at controlling the mind to binding the
mighty wind. Krishna's reply acknowledged
the hazard involved and at the same time struck
a positive and optimistic note. It is a slow,
steady and prolonged process. 'Watch and
wait' is its watchword. The secret of success
lies in patience and steadiness. In spiritual
life, the method is more important than the
end. Once the end is fixed on, one can forget
it ; the whole attention may then be directed
to the means. The sustained struggle itself is
practically the end so far as an aspirant is concerned.

The monkey has to be taught to obey the
bidding of the master. Mind has to be made
aware that it is only a servant and that the
master is someone above it. In the path of
knowledge, the mind is required to dwell on
the Ultimate, incomprehensible Reality. By
definition, the Ultimate Reality is beyond
mind. To assign the mind to grasp the infinite

is asking for the impossible. Even the wise lose their way in that path, says the Bhagavata. Patanjali's path, though very systematic, is difficult of attainment, for it is almost impossible to possess all the prerequisites. It is a frontal encounter with the mind. Either it plays truant or cracks. The *Bhagavata* has a smooth and effective way for the purpose.

Concentration is the essence of meditation. It is well known that the mind gets easily concentrated on matters of its liking. Objects of the senses are charming and the mind naturally flows towards them. Give it something more charming and it will automatically flow in that direction. Instead of trying to stem a strong current abruptly, cut a channel on the upper reaches and divert the flow through it, and you can regulate the water to turn a turbine to produce light and power. That is the method that the *Bhagavata* proposes and hence its popular appeal. That takes into account the neeeds and limitations of the mind, and therefore it is a truly psychological approach.

> *Asti bhāti priyam rūpam*
> *nāma ca ityamśa-pancakam*
> *ādya-trayam brahma-rūpam*
> *jagad-rūpam tato dvayam*

Being, knowing, bliss, form and name are
the five constituents of the Totality. The
first three are Brahman and the last two the
changing world. Philosophically the world
is called Maya. Mind is Maya individualised.
It operates in the *mayic* field. Its field is the
phenomenal world. Endow Brahman with
a *mayic* cover and the mind will apprehend
it. Invest the Satchidananda with a name
and a form and the mind can grasp it. That
is why Narada instructed Vyasa, the author
of the *Brahmasutras* to sing the glories of the
Incarnations of God. The *Bhagavata* provides innumerable forms of God for meditation, all sublime and enchanting. Not only
that, it allows free play to all human emotions.
Emotion directed to divinity is devotion. The
Bhagavata approves of establishing any kind
of emotional relation with divinity ; paternal
or maternal, fraternal or filial, erotic or esoteric
relations to the divine are adopted. Nay even
an antagonistic way to God is recognised. All
the demons of the *Bhagavata* are deeply devoted
to God and their apparent antagonism is an
expression of their impatience to go back to the
feet of God. In intensity of feeling, perhaps
they may rank on a par with the bucolic lasses
of Vrindaban. The advantage in adopting an

emotional and personal relation to God is
that the mind will dwell on Him constantly
without cessation. It will be spontaneous,
smooth and incessant meditation. The devotee
dwells ever in the presence of God. There is
no formality in this path. It is meditation
with eyes open. Wherever his eyes set, there
he espies his Beloved. The Gopis were always
in sublime peace, a state of divine intoxication. Suka was ever in bliss, Narada was
at all times in divine inebriation. Prahlada
was soaked in bliss divine for ever. Mira, the
great saintly singer, is said to have been brought
up by her grandparents as she lost her parents
early in life. Her grandfather was a devout
man. He used to sing and dance in the name
of God and lose himself in meditation. The
little girl was fascinated and perplexed. She
asked her grandpa why he was shouting and
jumping at times and sitting like a stock at
other times. How to explain the mysteries
of devotion to a tiny tot? He said he was
praying and meditating. What is praying, and
what is meditating, demanded Mira. Her
grandpa said : 'When we talk to God,
it is prayer and when God talks to us, it is
meditation'. Mira's whole life was a continuous
dialogue between her Soul and her Beloved.

Well, Mira's way is the *Bhagavata* way, a
continuous pre-occupation of the Soul with
God. The afflicted man, when at his wit's
end, turns to God and pours out his worries
and cares, submits his complaints and prays
for succour. That is the stage of the Soul
speaking to God. When man feels utterly
helpless and cries quarter, God opens his portals
and man remains mute. These are the various
stages of meditation.

In Book XI. Ch. 23 of the *Bhagavata* there
is the story of a Brahmana, who was miserliness
personified and hated by one and all. Fate
deprived him of all his wealth, and he became
a mendicant and was insulted and tortured by
the people. Learning his lesson through
bitter experiences, he became cool and
composed. There is a beautiful philsophical
passage attributed to him. Among other
things he says : 'These people are not the
cause of my misery, nor the angels nor God,
nor the stars, nor fate nor time. Mind is the
prime cause and the whole wheel of life turns
and twirls because of the mind. It sets in
motion the strong desires. The Jiva embraces
the mind and gets entangled and enchained
in worldly affairs. All spiritual disciplines
such as fasts and vigils, charity and dutifulness

purity and poverty, all these have only one
goal in view, namely the control of the mind :
for, the highest Yoga is concentration of the
mind. If once the mind is controlled, of what
use are charity and other virtues ? And if
the mind is not under control, what availeth
one the observance of charity, poverty and
the like ? All the gods are under the control
of the mind; the mind is not under the control
of anyone. Mind is a terrible god, stronger
than the strongest. He who has it under his
control is verily the God of gods. Without
subjugating this relentless foe, man falls foul
of fellow-men. Identifying himself with the
body which is nothing but a mental construct,
he roams about deluded in this endless darkness. I shall take to the path the ancient sages
have trodden. I shall serve the Lord's feet
and shall cross this shoreless ocean of Samsara.'

The normal haunts of the mind are the world
of the senses. Give it something better and
sweeter and it will take to it.

> *Viṣayān dhyāyataścittam*
> *viṣayeṣu viṣajjate*
> *mām anusmarataścittam*
> *mayi eva pravilīyate*
>
> *Bh*. XI. 14. 27.

'The mind that dwells on sense-objects gets
stuck in them. The mind that remembers
Me constantly, gets dissolved in Me,' says
Krishna to Uddhava. That is the mode of
meditation advocated by the *Bhagavata*. Ordi-
narily, meditation is the despair of aspirants,
for, the mind does not relish any sort of restraint. But then, sweeten the emotion with
devotion, and meditation becomes sweet and
spontaneous. Prahlada told his friends: 'It
isn't very difficult to please the Lord, for He
is within one and all and is visible everywhere.'
He was looking through the eyes of love. When
his teachers asked him who turned his head
to Hari, Prahlada replied : 'As the iron
filings fly to the magnet, so does my mind run
to the feet of the Wielder of the discus.' When
meditation is cultured in the medium of love,
it is easy, sweet and lovely. Then look anywhere, you will see the wonder child of Vraja
playing around. Tune your soul to Vrindaban,
you will hear the sweet strains from Krishna's
flute. If only you love Him sufficiently, you
can constantly live and play with Him.

> *Komalam kūjayan veṇum*
> *śyamaloyam kumārakaḥ*
> *vedavedyam param brahma*
> *bhāsatām purato mama*

' May He of hue welkin-blue, He, the Supreme Soul of all the Vedas, dance before me playing on His divine flute '. That is the prayer of the devotee : that is the vision he craves for. And that is the meditation according to the *Bhagavata,* a sweet and constant awareness of the ever playful and the ever blissful Supreme Lord.

Attune your ears to Vrindaban like the Gopis ; you will hear the call of Krishna through his flute. Pluck at the lute of your heart with loving abandon, like Narada ; Hari will come running into your heart. Open your Soul to the Lord like Prahlada ; you will see Hari everywhere. Meditate on the Lord like Sri Suka and you are ever in the presence of God.

The finale of meditation is spiritual illumination and its language is silence. A peace that passeth understanding is its subjective content and an irenic, elusive smile, its visible indication. ' Silence is Brahman ' say the Seers.

MEDITATION ACCORDING TO SWAMI VIVEKANANDA

By

SWAMI ANANYANANDA

Introduction

It is being increasingly recognized by modern psychologists that meditation should form part and parcel of the daily life and routine of man, in order to provide a counter-balance to the intensely active mode of life he lives in the pretent-day world. Meditation calms the mind, brings self-composure, and enables one to concentrate one's mental powers. By self-conscious effort, one can develop those virtues and graces that bring affection in human hearts, smoothen their inter-relationships, and provide a sound basis for mutual amity and understanding. Last but not the least, regular practice of meditation enables men and women to bend their energies in the pursuit of Truth and evertually to attain spiritual beatitude and the peace that passeth all understanding.

According to Swami Vivekananda, ' religion is the manifestation of the divinity already in man '. Meditation is the means and the method by which the soul unveils the layers of ignorance covering it and discovers the essen‐ tial divinity of its own being, by a three‐fold process of *śravaṇa* (hearing), *manana* (reflec‐ tion), and *nididhyāsana* (meditation), being equipped with what is known as *sadhana cha‐ tushtaya* (four‐fold pre‐requisites of spiritual life). This can be described as spiritual un‐ foldment leading to Self‐knowledge. This, however, is the language of the *jnani* or Vedan‐ tin (philosopher treading the path of knowledge or *jnana*).

In the language of the *bhakta* (devotee), meditation is a process in which the individual soul pours out its own being into the divine, like the unbroken flow of oil poured from one vessel to another, and empties itself in the latter, as the river flowing into the sea. It finds itself safe and secure under the protection of the divine, in being held fast in the bosom of the divine. In this case, meditation acts as a link to establish a connection between the individual soul (*jivatman*) and the Super Soul (*Para‐ matman*).

What Is Meditation ?

' What is meditation ? ' asks Swami Vivekananda, and answers himself : ' Meditation
is the power which enables us to resist all this
(manifold manifestation of alluring names
and forms, which distract our minds
from our chosen path). Nature may
call us, " Look, there is a beautiful thing ! "
I do not look. Now she says " There is a
beautiful smell ; smell it ! " I say to my nose,
" Do not smell it ", and the nose doesn't.
" Eyes, do not see ! " Nature does such an
awful thing — kills one of my children and
says, " Now, rascal, sit down and weep ! Go
to the depths ! " I say, " I don't have to ". I
jump up. I must be free. Try it sometimes.
In meditation, for a moment, you can change
your nature. Now, if you had that power in
yourself, would not that be heaven, freedom?
That is the power of meditation '. (*The Complete Works of Swami Vivekananda*, IV, p. 248).

' How is it to be attained ? In a dozen
different ways. Each temperament has its
own way. But this is the general principle :
get hold of the mind. The mind is like a lake,
and every stone that drops into it raises waves.
These waves do not let us see what we are.

The full moon is reflected in the water of the lake, but the surface is so disturbed that we do not see the reflection clearly. Let it be calm. Do not let nature raise the wave. Keep quiet, and then after a little while she will give you up. Then we know what we are. God is there already, but the mind is so agitated, always running after the senses. You close the senses, and yet you whirl and whirl about '. (*ibid*).

Meditation is concentration of mind and its innate powers. The untrained mind is scattered (*vikshipta*), as it runs after every sensation obtained through the sense organs. The mind needs to be weaned from those contacts with the senses and then collected together, concentrated into a single force, and directed towards a lofty object that is pure, holy, and spiritually uplifting — no matter whether it is personal or impersonal. Swamiji says : " Meditation is the gate that opens that (infinite joy) to us. Prayers, ceremonials, and all other forms of worship are simply kindergartens of meditation. You pray ; you offer something. A certain theory existed that everything raised one's spiritual power. The use of certain words, flowers, lights brings the mind to that attitude,

but that attitude is always in the human soul,
nowhere else. People are all doing it ; but
what they do without knowing, do know-
ingly. That is the power of meditation ".
(*ibid.,* p. 249).

The embodied soul has forgotten its real
nature. Rather, it is not aware of it. By
concentration and meditation, the soul can
realize its true nature. One of the methods
advocated is the purification of thought, word,
and deed (*trikarana-suddhi*). It is a slow and
gradual process. It sounds funny, but none
the less cannot be denied, that whenever we
try to sit quiet and collect our mind, and think
of concentrating it on some elevating ideal,
our mind rebels and refuses to obey at first,
and flies here, there, and everywhere, except
to the object of concentration.

Swamiji portrays to us the pitiable plight
of this 'maddened monkey' in his *Rajayoga* :
' How hard it is to control the mind! Well
has it been compared to the maddened monkey.
There was a monkey, restless by his own nature,
as all monkeys are. As if that were not enough,
some one made him drink freely of wine, so
that he became still more restless. Then a
scorpion stung him. When a man is stung

by a scorpion, he jumps about for a whole day: so the poor monkey found his condition worse than ever. To complete his misery, a demon entered into him. What language can describe the uncontrollable restlessness of that monkey? The human mind is like that monkey, incessantly active by its own nature; then it becomes drunk with the wine of desire, thus increasing its turbulence. After desire takes possession comes the sting of the scorpion of jealousy at the success of others, and last of all the demon of pride enters the mind, making it think itself of all importance. How hard to control such a mind !' (*C.W.*, I, p. 174).

In order to succeed in this task of controlling the mind and attaining concentration on a particular object that is spiritually elevating, Swamiji's prescription is *pratyāhāra,* which he describes in these words: ' The first lesson, then, is to sit for some time and let the mind run on. The mind is bubbling all the time. It is like the monkey jumping about. Let the monkey jump as much as he can; you simply wait and watch. Knowledge is power, says the proverb, and that is true. Until you know what the mind is doing, you cannot control it. Give it the rein; many hideous thoughts may

come into it; and you will be astonished that
it was possible for you to think such thoughts.
But you will find that each day the mind's
vagaries are becoming less and less violent,
that each day it is becoming calmer. In the
first few months, you will find that the mind
will have a great many thoughts ; later, you
will find that they have somewhat decreased;
and in a few more months, they will be fewer,
until at last the mind will be under prefect control, but we must patiently practise every day.
As soon as the steam is turned on, the engine
must run; as soon as things are before us, we
must perceive ; so a man, to prove that he is
not a machine, must demonstrate that he is
under the control of nothing. This controlling
of the mind and not allowing it to join itself to
the centres is *pratyāhāra*. How is this
practised ? It is a tremendous work, not to be
done in a day. Only after a patient, continuous
struggle for years can we succeed ' (*C.W.*, I.
pp. 174–75).

The Object of Meditation

Commenting on the sutra '*Yathābhima-
tadhyānādvā*' (Yoga-Sutra, I, 39), 'Or by the
meditation on anything that appeals to one as

good ', Swamiji warns us: 'This does not mean any wicked subject, but anything good that you like, any place that you like best, any scenery that you like best, any idea that you like best, anything that will concentrate the mind ' (*C.W.*, pp. 227–28).

Stating that there are various stages of meditation, he points out how the first would be the gross, the second the fine, and then on to the still finer objects. The objects of meditation can be both, personal and impersonal. If it be personal, usually it is the form of a god or a goddess, an Incarnation of God or a god-man, or a perfected being who has attained the consummation of spiritual life. The name and form of such beings play an important role in the process of meditation. Contemplation on the form (*rūpa*) of the chosen ideal (*ishta-devatā*) and repetition of the name (*nāma*) of that being constitute the essential acts of meditation of the personal type. The need of a guru (spiritual teacher) is considered to be the *sine qua non* in this method.

There is also an impersonal form, a symbol, regarded as most sacred and ancient, which has come down to us from the dim ages of Vedic antiquity, and is still held in high venera-

tion and as holy by all the religious sects and
schools in India. It is the sacred mono-syllable
Aum, popularly written as *Om.* Swamiji con-
siders it the 'holiest of all holy words, the
mother of all names and forms' (*C. W.* III. p. 57).
He goes on to say, 'the whole universe may be
supposed to have been created' out of this
eternal *Om* (*ibid.*)

' *Om* is the only possible symbol which covers
the whole ground, and there is none other like
it. .... If properly pronounced, this *Om*
will represent the whole phenomenon of sound-
production, and no other word can do this;
and this, therefore, is the fittest symbol of
Sphota, which is the real meaning of the *Om.*
And as the symbol can never be separated from
the thing signified, the *Om* and the Sphota are
one. And as the Sphota, being the finer side
of the manifested universe, is nearer to God
and is indeed the first manifestation of divine
wisdom, this *Om* is truly symbolic of God'
(*ibid.,* pp. 57–58).

Again : ' These word-symbols, evolved out
of the deepest spiritual perception of sages,
symbolize and express, as nearly as possible
the particular view of God and the universe
they stand for. And as the *Om* represents the

Akhanda, the undifferentiated Brahman, the others represent the Khanda or the differentiated views of the same Being ; and they are all helpful to divine meditation and the acquisition of pure knowledge ' (*ibid.*, p. 59).

In the light of what has been stated above, we can really understand the unique position accorded to the *mantra* (sacred name of a god or formula) and the *japa* (its repetition) in the different religious systems and spiritual practices the world over.

In this context, it is worthwhile to recall the *Yoga-Sutra* (I. 28), '*Tajjapastadarthabhā-vanam*' — 'The repetition of this (*Om*) and meditation on its meaning (is the way)' Explaining this *sutra*, Swamiji says : ' Why should there be repetition ? We have not forgotten the theory of *samskāras,* that the sum total of impressions lives in the mind. They become more and more latent, but remain there ; and as soon as they get the right stimulus they come out, molecular vibration never ceases ...... When the vibrations of the *chitta* subside, its molecular vibrations go on ; and when they get the impulse, come out again. We can now understand what is meant by repetition. It is the greatest stimulus that can be

given to the spiritual *samskāras*. " One
moment of company with the holy makes a
ship to cross this ocean of life". Such is the
power of association. So this repetition of
Om, and thinking of its meaning, is keeping
good company in your own mind. Study,
and then meditate on what you have studied.
Thus light will come to you ; the Self will
become manifest ' (*C.W.,* I.pp. 219–20).

Aids to Meditation

An aspirant needs a conducive and congenial
environment to practise meditation. Swamiji's
advice is: 'Those of you who can afford it will
do better to have a room for this practice alone.
Do not sleep in that room ; it must be kept
holy. You must not enter the room until
you have bathed, and are perfectly clean in
body and mind. Place flowers in that room
always ; they are the best surrounding for a
Yogi; also pictures that are pleasing. Burn
incense morning and evening. Have no
quarrelling, nor anger, nor unholy thought in
that room. Only allow those persons to enter
it who are of the same thought as you. Then
gradually there will be an atmosphere of holiness
in the room, so that when you are miserable,

sorrowful, doubtful, or your mind is disturbed, the very fact of entering that room will make you calm ...... The idea is that by keeping holy vibrations there the place becomes and remains illumined. Those who cannot afford to have a room set apart can practise anywhere they like ' (*ibid.*, p. 145).

The *Bhagavad Gita* prescribes the *modus operandi* for meditation as follows in the sixth chapter, entitled ' Dhyana Yoga ' : ' Having set in a clean place his firm seat, neither too high nor too low, covered with sacred grass (*kuśa*) a deerskin, and a cloth, one over the other ; there taking his place on the seat, making his mind one-pointed and controlling his thought and sense, let him practise Yoga for the purification of the soul. Holding the body, head, and neck erect and still, looking fixedly at the tip of his nose, without looking around, serene and fearless, firm in the vow of celibacy (divine life), subdued in mind let him sit, harmonized, his mind turned to Me and intent on Me alone ' (VI.11–14).

In addition to the prescription of the *Gita* delineated above, we can profit by Swamiji's own suggestion also in this regard : ' Sit in a straight posture, and the first thing to do is to

send a current of holy thought to all creation.
Mentally repeat, " Let all beings be happy ;
let all beings be peaceful ; let all beings be
blissful ". So do to the East, South, North,
and West. The more you do that the better
you will feel yourself. .... After doing that,
those who believe in God should pray — not
for money, not for health, nor for heaven ;
pray for knowledge and light ; every other
prayer is selfish. Then the next thing to do
is to think of your own body, and see that it
is strong and healthy ; it is the best instrument
you have. Think of it as being as strong as
adamant, and that with the help of this body
you will cross the ocean of life. Freedom is
never to be reached by the weak. Throw away
all weakness. Tell your body that it is strong ;
tell your mind that it is strong; and have
unbounded faith and hope in yourself' (*C.W.*, I.
145–46).

Impediments to Meditation

It is relevant to quote here the warning
sounded by Swamiji to those who take to the
Yoga of meditation, out of curiosity and seeking
something mysterious out of it: " Anything
that is secret and mysterious in the systems of

Yoga should be at once rejected. The best guide in life is strength. In religion, as in other matters, discard everything that weakens you ; have nothing to do with it. Mystery-mongering weakens the human brain. It has well-nigh destroyed Yoga — one of the grandest of sciences. From the time it was discovered, more than four thousand years ago, Yoga was perfectly delineated, formulated, and preached in India. It is a strking fact that the more modern the commentator the greater the mistakes he makes, while the more ancient the writer the more rational he is. Most of the modern writers talk of all sorts of mystery. Thus Yoga fell into the hands of a few persons who made it a secret, instead of letting the full blaze of daylight and reason fall upon it. They did so that they might have the powers to themselves' (*ibid.*, p. 134.)

Pointing out the main aim of meditation, Swamiji remarks : ' Meditation is one of the great means of controlling the rising of these (thought) waves. By meditation, you can make the mind subdue these waves ; and if you go on practising meditation for days, and months, and years, until it has become a habit, until it will come in spite of yourself, anger and hatred will be controlled and checked' (*ibid.*, p. 242–43).

In each and every one of us, there are what are called six internal enemies. These are born with us : *kāma* (desire), *krodha* (*anger*), *lobha* (greed), *moha* (delusion), *mada* (*pride*), and *mātsarya* (jealousy). These are powerful impulses native to every embodied human being, and belong to the very flesh of humanity. Most often, we are under their sway ; we are helpless, as it were. To master them by keeping them under check and eventually to sublimate them is the aim of all spiritual struggle. In this, meditation and self-reflection will help us a great deal. This is the teaching of every religious system and every spiritual discipline : to sublimate them and derive help from them, and not to suppress them. Suppression may lead to undesirable consequences and psychological complications and disorders. Instead of helping one, such a situation may create unforeseen hindrances. Hence sublimation is advocated as the best means.

In this process of sublimation, meditation comes in handy and serves a very useful purpose. In short, spiritual life means the sublimation of these 'six internal enemies' which drag us out, lead us away from our set goal of perfection, and make us fritter away our vital energies for no earthly or heavenly benefit !

The *Yoga-Sutra* enumerates several impediments on the path of yoga: ' Disease, mental laziness, doubt, lack of enthusiasm, lethargy, clinging to sense-enjoyments, false perception, non-attaining concentration and falling away from the state when obtained, are the obstructing distractions ' (I. 30). Commenting on this *sutra,* Swamiji explains these distractions one by one : ' *Disease* — This body is the boat which will carry us to the other shore of the ocean of life. It must be taken care of. Unhealthy persons cannot be Yogis. *Mental laziness* makes us lose all lively interest in the subject, without which there will neither be the will nor the energy to practise. *Doubts* will arise in the mind about the truth of the science, however strong one's intellectual conviction may be, until certain peculiar psychic experiences come, as hearing or seeing at a distance etc. These glimpses strengthen the mind and make the student persevere. *Falling away from the state when obtained* — Some days or weeks when you are practising, the mind will be calm and easily concentrated,

and you will find yourself progressing fast.
All of a sudden, the progress will stop one day ;
and you will find yourself, as it were, stranded.
Persevere. All progress proceeds by such rise
and fall' (*C.W.*, I. p. 221).

Fruitful Meditation

The mind of man has a unique capacity,
which no other creature has. The human
mind operates on two levels — the higher and
the lower. The higher reflects divinity. It
is ennobling. The lower reflects animality.
It is degrading. Another feature of the human
mind, which has no parallel, is its inherent
quality of itself becoming both, the subject and
the object. It can play a dual role simultaneously ! The mind can, and does, divide
itself into two — objectify itself and study it
also. It is a curious mixture.

Human beings possess what is known as
conscience. It is this special possession of
man that warns him at critical times. But
man, as he is constituted, pays little or no heed
to the warnings or the gnawing of conscience.
The result is that, in spite of these warnings, he
indulges in wicked deeds and becomes more

and more roguish and vicious. He degrades
himself and becomes a curse to his fellowmen.
On the other hand, one who is wakeful to the
inner workings of one's mind and listens to the
voice within pays heed to the caution sounded
by this conscience in time. He guards himself
against possible pitfalls, conducting himself in
accordance with the established social moral
code. He engages himself in working for
the good and welfare of others among whom
he lives and functions. By such acts, he himself becomes noble and proves to be a blessing
to others as well. Let us listen to what Swamiji
has to say on this point : ' The mind uncontrolled and unguided will drag us down, down,
for ever — rend us, kill us ; and the mind controlled and guided will save us, free us ' (*C.W.*,
VI. p. 30).

Swamiji's advice to us is to meditate in silence.
About the power of silence, he says : ' Truth
cannot be partial ; it is for the good of all.
Finally, in perfect rest and peace, meditate
upon It ; concentrate your mind upon It ;
make yourself one with It. Then no speech is
needed ; silence will carry the truth. Do not
spend your energy in talking, but meditate in
silence ; and do not let the rush of the outside

world disturb you. When your mind is in the
highest state, you are unconscious of it. Accu-
mulate power in silence, and become a dynamo
of spirituality' (*C.W.*, pp. 60–61).

Be the witness ! That is the trumpet-call
of Swamiji, when he says : ' Say when the
tyrant hand is on your neck, " I am the Witness !
I am the Witness ! " Say, " I am the Spirit !
Nothing external can touch me. " When evil
thoughts arise, repeat that, give that sledge-
hammer blow on their heads, " I am the Spirit !
I am the Witness, the Everblessed ! " I have
no reason to do; no reason to suffer; I have
finished with everything ; I am the Witness '
(*C.W.*, V. p. 254).

Further : "It is all play. .... Play ! God
Almighty plays. That is all. .... You are
the almighty God playing. ....It is all fun.
Know it and play. That is all there is to it.
Then practise it. The whole universe is a vast
play. All is good because all is fun. ....Do
not be miserable! Do not repent: What
is done is done. If you burn yourself take the
consequences. ......Be sensible. We make
mistakes ; what of that? That is all in fun.
They go so crazy over their past sins, moaning
and weeping and all that. Do not repent!

After having done work, do not think of it. Go on ! Stop not ! Don't look back! What will you gain by looking back ?" (*C.W.*, II. pp. 470–71).

Let us close this exposition with Swamiji's own immortal and inspiring exhortation: ' Arise ! Awake ! And stop not till the goal is reached. '

———

MEDITATION ACCORDING TO PATANJALI

SWAMI HARSHANANDA

The diffused rays of the sun, when gathered to a point by a convex lens, can start a devastating fire. A powerful searchlight can reveal any object, towards which it is turned on. In the same way, when the forces of the mind, normally diffused or even confused, are gathered together and concentrated, can give us knowledge and power.

However, this concentration of mind involves a very arduous process. As in the case of any other science, art or craft, this also has to be learnt from competent teachers and practised assiduously. One of the all-time great teachers of this science and art, is the sage Patañjali. His " Yoga Sutras " is a basic text embodying a systematic treatment of this subject.

As in the case of other Indian philosophical systems, here also *kaivalya* or liberation is set forth as the goal of life. But unlike, in those systems, Patañjali cares little for philosophical disquisitions and goes straight to the practical means of achieving it. Mind being the chief means in this process, he has dealt with the subject of its composition, function and control. According to him, the mind is as much a product of the three *guṇas* (*sattva, rajas* and *tamas*) as the body or the external physical objects, though it has much finer vibrations. It normally functions in the form of *vṛttis* (waves or modifications).

Swami Vivekananda compares the mind to a lake. When the water of the lake is absolutely calm and steady, one can see the reflection of one's face in it, or a piece of stone lying at its bottom. When the water is disturbed by waves, this will not be possible. In the same way when our mind is rising in the form of *vṛttis* it is not possible to get a true picture of our real self. If and when, as a result of practising yoga, we successfully eliminate all the *vṛttis*, we will certainly have a vision of our true self, the spirit behind our mind, our personality.

Patanjali defines yoga as *citta-vṛittinirodha,* suppression of the modifications of the mind. Since these *vṛttis* are innumerable, will it ever be possible to control them and suppress them ? Patañjali being endowed with a practical and

scientific attitude, assures us that it is possible
to do so. How ? Though, individually, there
appear to be any number of these *vṛttis* cate-
gorywise there are only five ! He classifies
them as : *pramāṇa* (true cognition), *viparyaya*
(false cognition), *vikalpa* (verbal cognitions),
nidrā (deep sleep) and *smṛti* (memory).

Pratyakṣa (direct perception), *anumāna* (in-
ference) and *āgama* (verbal testimony or scriptural testimony) constitute true cognition. False
cognition is wrong knowledge of things, and
includes doubts as also uncertain cognitions.
Verbal cognition arises by hearing a word which
has no corresponding reality. Sleep stands for
dreamless sleep and is due to the preponderance
of *tamas* in the *citta*, which *tamas* is the cause
of absence of ordinary perception at that time.
Memory is the reproduction of past experiences
without any alteration or innovation. All
other cognitive mental states can be included
under these heads.

After conceding the possibility of controlling
and suppressing these mental modifications,
Patañjali reveals the age-old (open ?) secret
of achieving this : *abhyāsa* (repeated practice)
and *vairāgya* (dispassion).

The tremendous energy of the waters of a river is wasted when it flows wildly, often bringing untold sufferings to the people living on its banks. When a dam is constructed across it, this energy is conserved. It is then guided through channels and canals or pipes for irrigation or generation of power. In exactly the same way the mad rush of the mental energies which are being wasted through the senseless enjoyment of sensual pleasures must be halted by cultivating dispassion towards these sense objects and the energies thus saved should be directed towards the self or God within. *Vairāgya* and *abhyāsa* mean just this and nothing more ! However Patañjali advises us to practise yoga constantly, continuously and with feeling, and warns us not to expect quick results!

Man by nature is averse to hard and sustained effort. He always seeks for short-cuts. Hence Patañjali provides for that too ! He declares out of infinite compassion for mankind, that by devotion and self-surrender to God (*Iśvarapraṇidhāna*) one can get complete control over the mind resulting ultimately even in *samādhi* (super-conscious experience).

Any person who wishes to have a strong

and healthy body, must have a basic know
ledge of diseases which destroy this health
After all, prevention is better than cure ! So
anyone desirous of practising yoga, must b
aware of the obstacles to yoga so that they cai
be avoided or remedied. Patañjali lists 9 obsta
cles to yoga : (1) *vyādhi* (physical sickness)
(2) *styāna* (languor) ; (3) *samśaya* (doubts
and misgivings) ; (4) *pramāda* (heedlessness) ;
(5) *ālasya* (sloth) ; (6) *avirati* (absence of dispassion) ; (7) *bhrāntidarśana* (hallucinations);
(8) *alabdhabhūmikatva* (non-attainment of the
stage of communion in spite of effort) ; (9)
anavasthitatva (instability).

Vyādhi should be overcome by proper medi.
cines, treatment and diet, *styāna* by discrimination and will-power, *samśaya* by faith in the
scripture, the guru and oneself *pramāda* by
eternal vigilance, *ālasya* by healthy physical
activity, *avirati* by reflecting on the transient
and evil nature of sense-pleasures and *bhrāntidarśana* by right perception. The last two,
viz., *alabdha-bhūmikatva* and *anavasthitatva*
are more serious obstacles encountered in the
higher stages of *sādhanā*. Just as rat-holes
in an agricultural field drain away all water.
in the same way, deep-rooted evil *samskāras*

(impressions left over by past-life experiences) nullify all efforts at spiritual progress. Guidance from the Guru or advanced souls as also prayer and self-analysis will help to locate and eradicate these *saṁskāras*.

This preliminary knowledge should suffice the beginning of yogic practice which itself consists of eight graded steps: 1. *yama* (restraint): 2. *niyama* (culture): 3. *āsana* (posture): 4. *prāṇāyāma* (control of psychic *prāna*): 5. *pratyāhāra* (withdrawal of senses): 6. *dhāraṇā* (fixed attention): 7. *dhyāna* (meditation): 8. *samādhi* (perfect concentration resulting in super-conscious experience).

Yama is a moral discipline and consists of: *ahiṁsā* abstention from all kinds of injury to life; *satya* (truthfulness in thought, word and deed); *asteya* (non-stealing); *brahma-carya* (control of carnal passions) and *aparigraha* (non-acceptance of gifts, more than necessary for sustenance).

Niyama consists in cultivating *śauca* (cleanliness), *santoṣa* (contentment), *tapas* (austerity of body, speech and mind), *svādhyāya* (study of scriptures) and *iśvara-praṇidhāna* (surrendering the fruits of actions to God).

It is to be noted here that *yama* and *niyama*, the basic ethical disciplines, have been placed at the very foot of the ladder of yogic ascension. This implies that those who have not given up evil ways of life, cannot aspire to become yogis! Misdeeds and meditation cannot co-exist!

Āsana is a discipline of the body, and consists in the adoption of steady and comfortable postures for the sake of meditation. This is achieved through releasing the physical and mental tensions and through the contemplation on the *ananta,* the infinite sky. The steadiness of the body thus achieved is conducive to the steady flow of mind towards the ideal.

An excited mind throws the breathing out of rhythm. A calm and quiet mind, on the other hand, is invariably accompanied by rhythmic breathing. This fact from our experience gives us a very useful and practical hint to control the mind. Practice of rhythmic breathing, and even stopping the breath for some time in a systematic way, will help bring the mind under control. This is exactly the principle behind *prāṇā-yāma*. *Prāṇa* is actually the life-force permeating the whole world and manifests itself in our bodies as the bio-chemical and nervous energy. This energy is connected with the breath on the one side and with the mind on the other. Hence, control and regulation of breath gradually leads to the control and regulation of the mind itself. The process itself consists of *recaka* (exhalation), *pūraka* (inhalation) and *kumbhaka* (retention), in certain fixed proportions.

It is interesting to note that the great sage Patanjali has finished all about *āsana* and *prāṇāyama,* about which so much fuss is often made, in only eight *sūtras*. It must be remembered that the object of practising these two disciplines as also the others, is to obtain *samādhi* and that one gets a right to practise them only after scrupulously following moral discipline and culture as enjoined by *yama* and *niyama*.

The next step is *Pratyāhāra*, the withdrawal of senses from their respective external objects, keeping them under the control of the mind. When the senses are effectively controlled, they follow not their objects, but the mind itself. So, in this state, the mind is not disturbed by sights and sounds coming

5.

through the eyes and the ears, but makes these senses follow itself, and see and hear its own object.

These five disciplines are regarded as *bahiranga-sādhana* (external sides) of yoga, whereas the next three, (*dhāraṇā, dhyāna* and *samādhi*, are classified as *antaranga-sādhana* (internal means).

Dhāraṇā is the fixing of attention on a definite locus, such as the lotus of the heart, the light in the brain, the tip of the nose or the tongue, or on an external object like the moon or the image of gods and so on.

When *dhāraṇā* ripens so that the flow of the thought-current becomes unbroken, it becomes *dhyāna*. Here the mind hovers round the object of meditation. There is still the consciousness of the trio—the ego-sense, the object of meditation and the process of meditation.

When again *dhyāna* becomes perfect and the mind is so deeply absorbed in the object that it loses itself and has no awareness of itself, the state attained is called *samādhi*. In this state, only the object of meditation wil.

be shining in the mind and the yogi is not even aware of the thought process involved in it. Even the ego-sense is completely subjugated.

In the state of *samādhi*, which is an intuitive and superconscious experience, the object of meditation will reveal all its secrets to the yogi. If the yogi can make his own self or *Iśvara* the object of meditation after learning about them from the *Sāṅkhya* (an allied philosophical system declaring the knowledge of the self as the means of liberation), he will get *kaivalya* (liberation). Patañjali calls these two *sāmādhis* respectively, as *samprajñāta* and *asamprajñāta*. In the former, the object of meditation is known in its entirety. In the latter, nothing outside the self is known (*samprajñāta*=well known, *asamprajñāta*=not known).

This process of yoga and meditation as prescribed by Patañjali can be easily adopted to the path of Bhakti also. In the latter case, the *iṣṭadevatā* (the chosen deity) becomes the object of meditation.

MEDITATION ACCORDING TO YOGAVASISHTHA

Prof. B. Kuppuswamy

1. *Assumptions of Vasishtha*

According to the *Vāsishtha,* Brahman, the Absolute, manifests itself in the world. Everÿthing originates out of, exists in and finally merges into, the Brahman. He gives the analogy of the waves in the ocean. The waves arise, exist, and merge into the ocean. The difference between the world and the Brahman is due to ignorance and will cease to be believed in the enlightened state (VI-a. 49. 32). Similarly he held that the mind is not different from the Absolute. The limited and relative forms called the mind originate from and merge into the Brahman (III. 100.23). Again, according to Vasishtha every object of the world is the being of consciousness and the being of consciousness is the being of the world (III. 14.74).

The second assumption of Vasishtha is that

all living beings and all human beings, strive for happiness (VI. 188.20). The only trouble is that we seek happiness in wrong places. The animals and many human beings seek happiness by satisfying the bodily needs and by striving for sense-joys. However, the sense-enjoyments are pleasant only at the beginning. They have an inevitable end (V. 22.30). All pleasures terminate in pain (V. 49.6). Freud, the great psychoanalyst, called this the pursuit of *pleasure-principle,* typical of children. Vasishtha asserts that things by themselves are neither pleasant nor unpleasant. It is our attitude towards the objects and experiences that make them agreeable or disagreeable. The same object, say a sweet, is very pleasant when one starts eating. But with more of them, disgust towards them ensues (VI-a. 44.2-3).

So, Vasishtha concludes that when all desires are given up by the heart one experiences joy within (V. 74.24). One must give up notions like 'may this be mine' and 'may this not come to me.' In other words, real happiness arises with self-realization. It arises when the mind is at peace; that is, when the

mind is not functioning at the level of 'wants'
and 'don'ts'.

2. *Manas, Karma and Vasana*

Manas, mind, is ever-active like the
ripples in the motionless ocean. The ocean is
like the *chit,* the pure consciousness, or
Brahman. That is, the *chitta,* the mind, has
evolved from the *chit,* the pure consciousness.
The nature of manas is *karma,* activity. Thus
according to Vasishtha, karma is nothing
but the activity of the manas. Each activity
of manas is determined by its preceding
activity and determines, in its turn, the suc-
ceeding activity. Thus the cessation of
karma leads to the cessation of manas—
karma nāśe mano-nāśaḥ (III. 95). This is the
unique theory of Karma of Vasishtha, namely
that Karma is mental activity. According to
him, when *manas* arises from Brahman,
karma also arises simultaneously (III. 95.
1-12). That is, it is impossible to conceive of
manas without *karma.* The two are the
same. According to Vasishtha the terms
manas, chitta, vāsanā, and *karma* refer to the
same. They are merely varied names (II. 9.
13-21).

What about *vāsanā*? *Vāsanā* is the root desire, the root inclination in the *manas*. All action or active agency is associated with *vāsanā*. It is the presence of *vāsanā* that brings about the sense of agency, *kartṛtva* and sense of enjoyment, *bhoktṛtva*. Those who are free from *vāsanā* are free from attachment. They are active without being attached to the fruit of activity. That is, *vāsanā* and *karma* are, as Dasgupta (History of Indian Philosophy Vol. II, 1932) puts it, "more or less like the potential and actual states of the same activity" (p. 255). Vasishtha assumes that there are two distinct groups of *vāsanās* operating in the *manas*, one leading to the good of the individual and the group and the other leading to the evil of the individual and the group. It is the duty and the task of the individual to rouse the good *vāsanās* and overcome the evil *vāsanās*. (II. 9.25-31). It is Vasishtha's conviction that man is a free agent and it is for him to choose the course of action which contributes to his own good and the good of the group in which he lives.

3. *Prāṇa and its control*

According to Vasishtha, the *chitta* trans-

forms itself into *cittavṛttis,* the mental
states or mental modifications, due to two
reasons. One of these is the *parispanda,*
the vibration of the *prāṇa.* The other is the
vāsanā, the strong and deep-rooted desires
and inclinations. It is the *prāṇa-spandana,*
the vibration of the *prāṇa,* that leads to the
manifestation of the thoughts and the world-
appearance. Consequently, the cessation of
the vibration of *prāṇa* means the cessation of
all cognitive functions. There is also a close
relationship between *prāṇa-spanda* and
vāsanā. Prāṇa is set in motion through
vasana and *vasana* is created and stimulated
into activity by *prāṇa-spanda.* The cessation
of the *chitta,* the cessation of all the cognitive
functions, is possible through *prāṇāyāma,* regulation of breath and *dhyāna,* meditation. (V 91.
20-27).

In the purvardha of the Nirvana Prakarana, Vasishtha relates the story of Kaka
Bhusunda (VI.a. Chs. 24-26). Bhusunda is
the venerable old crow, who instructs Vasishtha about *prāṇa.* The body is compared
to a house and *ahamkāra,* the ego, to the
householder. A description is given of *rechaka,*
the outgoing breath, *puraka,* the breathing

in and *kumbhaka,* the interval between the two. Also there is a description of the two *nāḍis, iḍā* and *pingalā,* the left and right columns of the spinal cord with *sushumnā* in the centre. There is also the statement that the *prāṇa* forces are responsible for the breathing, the movement of the eyes, the digestion of food and the power of speech (VIa. 25. 6-11). Dasgupta observes, "It is curious to note in this connection that in the whole literature of the Ayurveda, there is probably no passage where there is such a clear description of the respiratory process"(ibid. p. 258 footnote).It is asserted that when there is cessation of the two operations of breathing in and breathing out, there is an unbroken continuity of *kumbhaka.* There is also the assertion that all the functions of breathing are due to the movement of *chitta* (VIa. 25. 61-74). Earlier it is said that *chitta* and the movement of the breath and body are one and the same, inseparable like the snow and its whiteness (V. ch. 78).

It is said that there are two ways of destroying the chitta, one by the cessation of mental states through *prāṇāyāma,* and the other by right knowledge. From the movement of *prana,* there is the movement of the *chitta* and from the movement of the *chitta* there is knowledge, *samvid*.

The control of the movement of *prāṇa* may be achieved through concentrating one's mind on one subject or through long inhalation associated with meditation or the practice of *kumbhaka*, retention of breath.

When Vasishtha asks Bhusunda to describe. the nature of *prāṇa vāyu*, he is informed that it is *spanda śakti*, the ever-moving vibration energy and that it functions in all the three states of waking, dream and deep sleep, that is, in all states of consciousness. It is said that all the three processes of inhalation, exhalation and retention of breath, occur without any effort (VI a. 251-11). It is pointed out that the person who pays attention to these three processes in a deliberate way is a Yogi. He gradually develops a contempt for all other activities and sense pleasures (VIa. 25. 20-24).

Bhusunda asserts that by resorting to *praṇa samādhi* in this manner, he was able to attain *chitta viśrānti*, mental peace. This is *ātma samādhi*. He experiences this peace whether he is stationary or moving about, whether he is awake, dreaming or asleep. He is in communion with the Absolute and is never concerned with the past or anxious about the future. He says that he will be in the *sushupti* state even while he is awake and active. (VI a. 26. 1-10). He has *samadrishti,* he looks on all as being equal. Whether it is a piece of wood (*kāshtam*) or a coquettish woman (*vilāsini*), a mountain or a blade of grass (*tṛṇa*), they are all the same. As a result, he says, he is ever happy. He further says that he never thinks of a person as a friend or relative(*bandhu*) or as an alien (*para*). He is able to look upon every one as the manifestation of the *chit,* the pure consciousness (VI. a. 26. 20-21). So he feels close, intimate and friendly towards every person. (VI a. 26. 34-35).

4. *Control of Mind*

According to Vasishtha, the World-experience is a delusion. He gives the analogy of the illusion of a circle of fire caused by the swinging round and round of torch (V. 78.1). As noted above, he asserts that there are two ways of overcoming this world delusion, namely, Yoga and Jnana. (V. 78.8). He asserts that Atmajnana, knowledge of self, leads to the control of mind. Jnana, he says,

consists in having the conviction that the
Absolute is beginningless (*anādi*) and endless
(*ananta*), that it is eternal and self-luminous.
When this *jnāna* arises, *ajnāna*, nescience is
destroyed. When *ajnāna* is destroyed there
is *mano-nāśa*, the destruction of the mind.
With it all the *manovṛttis,*the mental processes
and the experience of forms and perceptions,
automatically vanish. It is the mind that is
responsible for the functioning of the various
organs of sense and actions (the *jnānendriyas*
and *karmendriyas*). When there is control
over the mind, all the organs of sense and
action are automatically under control (V. 80.
15-20). Desires, then, will have no hold on one.
When the desires are not there, the question
of joys and sorrows does not arise at all (V.
80. 38-42).

When this Jnana arises, one is not disturbed
by the functioning of the mind. Experiences
will come and go in the manner of the
waves of the sea which arise and disappear
(V. 81. 11-14). In that condition, man has
neither the desire to acquire nor the desire
to reject. He becomes free from likes and
dislikes (V. 86. 10).

Some persons try to calm the mind with

the help of drugs. Vasishtha condemns these efforts. He also condemns the desire to acquire and exhibit *siddhis,* supernormal powers (V. 89. 12-16).

Vasishtha says that the *chitta-sattā,* the apparent reality of the mind, is responsible for world experience. So *chitta-nāśa,* the destruction of the mind leads to enlightenment. An enlightened person is not affected either by external or internal wants. He will be like a mountain that is unaffected by the winds. So long as one thinks about the seen (*the dṛśya*), he is steeped in foolishness.

Vasishtha told Rama that the world experience and the round of worldly activities (*samsara*) is due to the wheel of delusion (*maya chakra*); the hub of this wheel of delusion is the mind, the *chitta.* So the task of the individual is to utilize his intelligence or wisdom (*buddhi*) and make the mind stable. When the mind is stabilized through deliberate effort, the movement of the wheel of Maya will be arrested. When one attains that stability, all suffering and sorrow will vanish. It is *chitta nirodha,* the restraint of the mind, that is the supreme remedy for the disease of the wheel of worldly activities

(*samsāra*). When the mind, the *chitta*,
without being engaged in thinking of the
past and the future, is concerned with the
present in an effortless way and with detachment, then it becomes *achit,* free from concern
and anxiety. When the *chit,* the consciousness,
is free from *chitta,* the mind, it becomes *śud-
dhātmā,* pure self.

Rama asked Vasishtha to enlighten him
about the seed of worldliness (*samsāra bīja*).
The seed, he replies, is the body and the mind.
The sprout is the *vāsanā,* the impressions in
the mind which determine the further mental
processes and consequent woldliness. So that
supreme well-being (*śreyas*) consists in controlling the mental processes (*chitta vṛttis*).
When such control is attained, the seed will be
burnt (*dagdha bīja*) and powerless to sprout
(V. 91. 1-46). So long as the mind is active,
the *vāsanās,* the impressions, will be powerful.
When there is *mano nāśa* (the destruction of the
mind and mental concerns), *vāsanā kshaya*
will ensue. The past impressions and predelic-
tions will become powerless to influence the
conduct of the individual (V. 91.54-55).

Self-knowledge, the company of the
good, the relinquishment of predilictions,

the control of breath, are all necessary to attain victory over the mind (V. 92. 35-36).

This is why Vasishtha warns that mere control of the body through Hatha Yoga, without a control of the mind and without the attainment of self-knowledge, is futile (V. 92. 38-48).

According to Vasishtha the term Yoga stands for the practice in self-realisation. The term Yoga stands for (a) the deep affirmation of One Reality (*ekatattvatabhyāsaḥ*), (b) stopping the movement of the *prāṇas,* the vital currents (*prāṇānām vilayaḥ*) and (c) the control of mind (*manovinigrahaḥ*). (VIa. 69. 27). Success in any one of them leads to success in the others also. However, he prefers the control of mind as the easiest and the best. Of all the three methods of realisation, the control of mind is the best, because it is easily effected and leads to peace soon. (VI a. 69. 29).

Vasishtha is emphatic that the mind can be controlled and dissolved by one's own efforts and not by penances, pilgrimages, learning, sacrifices, etc. (VI b. 163:8). The important and effective means for control of the mind

is the eradication of egoistic feeling. Egoism
(*ahambhāva*) arises with the identification of
the self with some particular aspect of the
Infinite and the Absolute, whether it is the body,
or the family, or the nationality, etc. It is
ahamkāra, self-affirmation, that is the root of
the tree of mind. This has to be destroyed
(VI a. 94.13). This self-affirmation will die
when we realise that it is unreal from the point
of view of the Absolute. He asserts that when
the nature of the ego is known, it will vanish.
Let a man who is already peaceful, self-controlled
and free from sensual pleasures and selfish
desires, Vasishtha says, sit on a soft seat and
utter the *pranava,* Om, and feel that he is the
entire cosmos (VI a. 128. 1-25).

5.   *The seven stages of self-Realization*

Vasishtha describes the seven stages in
different sections: a) in the 118th chapter
of the third Prakarana, the Utpatti Prakarana, b) the 120th chapter of the purvardha
of Nirvana prakarana, and c) in the 126th
chapter of the same prakarana.

Putting them all together we can describe
the progressive path of the individual as he
ascends from particular conscious states to

the state of pure consciousness in the following way:

The first stage consists of *subhecchā,* the aspiration to transcend the worldly pre-occupations and engage himself in the study of the relevant books. The second stage consists in *vicharana,* critical inquiry regarding the nature of the self, the world and the Brahman. The third is the development of *asanga bhāvanā,* the affirmation of one's being detached from worldly pursuits and enjoyments. When *asanga* detachment, is cultivated, the aspirant will be peaceful and happy. The fourth stage is *vilapana,* in which all desires are annihilated. The fifth stage is that of *asamsakti,* in which one becomes detached from the objective world. As a result of this arises the sixth stage, *padārtha abhāvanā,* the realisation that the things of the world are unreal, that is, are not permanent. The seventh and final stage is that of *turīya,* the stage of liberation here and now, which is free from all agitations and is characterized by *samatva,* equanimity and *samadarśana,* looking on all persons with an equal eye. Such a person has no concern with differences in age, sex, status, etc. This is the stage of the *jivan-mukta,* the liberated man. The first three

stages correspond to the *jāgrat*, the waking state,
the fourth corresponds to the *svapna,* the dream
stage, and the fifth and sixth correspond to
the *sushupti* state, the state of deep sleep.
The last stage is the culmination, in which all
his desires, thoughts and actions have been
burnt up and so leave no *vāsanās*, no traces or
impressions, which generate further desires,
thoughts and actions.

6. *Concluding Remarks*

It is clear from the above that Vasishtha's
views regarding Yoga are quite different
from the views of Patanjali and others. As
noted above, he looks upon Yoga as the method
which enables one to transcend the finitude of
world-experience. *Samsarottaraṇe yuktiryo-
gaśabdena kathyate*—Yoga is the method of
crossing over the Samsara (VIa 13. 3). Jnana,
self-knowledge, is the only means for attaining
this. It is the conviction that Brahman alone
is the Reality. *Jnāna,* thus, is not a mere
intellectual affair. It is not mere knowledge.
In fact, he calls a man of knowledge a *Jnāna-
bandhu*. He is not a *Jnānin*. He asserts that a
Jnanabandhu is one who studies scriptures
merely to earn his livelihood. In this he is
like an artisan, a skilled craftsman, rather

than an artist. He does not make any effort to practise what he has learnt. His knowledge does not manifest itself in his actions. He just follows the injunctions of the Sruti. His aim is not self-realization. (VI b. 21. 3-8). The ideal of Yoga, according to Vasishtha, is to be in the *turiya* state, the fourth state, which is the realisation of bliss which is the nature of pure consciousness. (VI a. 128. 50-51).

As a result his emphasis is more on control of breath *prāṇāyāma*, control of the mind, *manovinigrahaḥ,* and the attainment of *jnāna* self-knowledge.

———

THE PLACE OF MEDITATION IN ADVAITA VEDANTA

DR. T. M. P. MAHADEVAN

Vedānta is not only a teaching of truth but also a way of life. The Upanishads which constitute Vedanta teach not only about the Reality referred to as *Brahman* or *Atman*, but they also prescribe in detail the methods by which *Brahman* is to be realized, i.e., to be experienced as the sole Reality. According to the Upanishads as expounded by Sankara: "The Absolute Spirit is the non-dual Reality; the world of phenomena is an illusion; the so-called individual soul is the Absolute Itself, and no other." The world appears to be real because of ignorance which binds the soul to the recurring cycle of birth and death. Knowledge of the non-dual *Brahman-Atman* (the Self free of limitations) effects release of the soul from restrictions superimposed on it, by removing ignorance. Release is only another name for the eternal Self (*Brahman-Atman*).

Release which is the goal as taught in the Upanishads is not what-is-to-accomplished. The expression that it is "attained" is but figurative and only from our limited standpoint of diversity. It is from this point of view that we say, knowledge must be "gained" etc. Actually knowledge is not acquired, for acquiring implies activity and anything caused by activity is by nature bound to be perishable.

It is true, however, that action may precede knowledge. For example one may act by turning the head towards the sun, but what is subsequently seen is not the result of an action but what is already there. In this sense, paths towards Release can be considered to consist of *karma,* disinterested service without expecting rewards, *bhakti,* devotion to a chosen Deity, and *jnana,* the way of inquiry. To follow the discipline of inquiry, which is the path of knowledge, certain qualifications are necessary. Sankara lays down these as the qualifications: Discrimination of the eternal from the non-eternal phenomena; non-attachment to the enjoyment of fruit (of endeavours) here or in a here-after; the possession in abundance of virtues such as calmness and equanimity, and the longing for release.

It is obvious that these qualifications of
eligibility to follow the path of knowledge
are difficult to obtain. What one should basi-
cally achieve is perfect mind-control. Mind-
control is achieved through concentration
and meditation. Meditation, it must be remembered, is a mental act and is different
from knowledge. It is prescribed for those
who are not yet ready for the path of knowledge. The benefit of meditation is that it
arrests the current of the mind which courses
its way to objects of sense, and causes it to
concentrate on *Brahman*. Meditation on *Brahman* may be compared to a delusion which
becomes fruitful. A delusion which yields a
fruitful result is called *samvadibhrama*. *visamva-
dibhrama,* its opposite, is a delusion which
does not lead to any fruitful consequence.
Let us illustrate this by an example: The
light of a lamp and the light of a gem may both
be mistaken for a gem. Both are cases of
delusion; but the person who mistakes the lamp
light for a gem, approaches but gains nothing;
while the one who mistakes the light of a gem
for a gem itself, gets the gem. Meditation on
Brahman is like the latter. There is meditation
on *Brahman* with attributes (*saguna*) and there
is also the meditation on *Brahman* without

attributes (*nirguṇa*). *Brahman* as such is unconditioned, without attributes, without qualifications (*nirguṇa*). It is the same Reality as endowed with attributes that is called God when viewed in relation to the empirical world and souls. *Brahman* is the same as *nirguṇa* (attributeless) and as *saguṇa* (with attributes). There are no two *Brahmans* as wrongly alleged by some critics. Even when God is referred to as the lower (*apara*) *Brahman,* what is meant is not that *Brahman* has become lower in status as God, but that God is *Brahman* looked at from the lower level of relative experience. These are two forms (*dvirupa*) of **Brahman** and not two *Brahmans; Brahman* as-It-is-in-Itself, and *Brahman* as-It-is-in-relation-to-the-world. The former is the unconditioned *Brahman,* the latter is *Brahman* as conditioned by nomenclature, configuration and change.

Superior to meditation on *Brahman* with attributes is meditation on *Brahman* without attributes. The criterion by which superiority of a particular method is determined is its relative proximity to *Brahman*-knowledge. Judged by this standard, meditation on the attributeless *Brahman* is superior to the remote methods like the performance of rites

and formal worship. Just as a delusion that
turns out to be fruitful becomes very much
like knowledge at the time of yielding fruit,
even so meditation on *Brahman* without attributes, when it matures, becomes like knowledge at the time of release.

Meditation on the attributeless *Brahman*
usually takes the form of meditation on the
sacred syllable *Om,* referred to as *praṇava*
Gaudapada, the illustrious predecessor of Sankara, explains the method of meditating on the
significance of *Om* in his verse commentary on
one of the Upanisads, the Mandukya-Upanisad.
Om is the sound which is indicative of *Brahman.*
It is inclusive of all sounds; and hence it is the
support of the world of speech (*vāk-prapañca*).
And of all that is denoted by sound, the ground
is *Brahman.* So, for purposes of meditation the
sound *Om* is made to stand for the Self or
Brahman. Of all the symbols, the sound *Om*
has come to be regarded as the most important
and fruitful. The Kathopanishad says, "The
word (or goal) which all the Vedas declare, that
which penances proclaim, and desiring which
people lead an austere life, that word (or goal)
I tell thee in brief: It is *Om.*" The Muṇḍako-
panishad compares the *praṇava* (the syllable

Om) to the bow, the individual soul to the arrow, and *Brahman* to the target, and says that the target is to be unerringly hit. Thus is union with *Brahman* attained. The fifth question of the Prasnopanishad relates to the meditation on *Om* as a means to the realization of the higher and the lower *Brahman*, i.e., the unconditioned *Brahman* and *Brahman* as conditioned. It is stated there that by means of *Omkāra* the wise one arrives at the Highest, which is quiescent and free from decay, death and fear.

The use of *Praṇava-dhyāna* or meditation on *Om* is, thus, well recognized in the Upanishads. In fact, the Mandukya starts by saying that its object is to expound the significance of *Omkāra*, and sketches the method of identifying the components of the sound "*Om*" with the aspects of the Self, and thereby realizing the truth of non-duality. There are four *mātrās* or morae of *Om* corresponding to the four phases of the Self. The four *mātrās* are a, u, m, and the fourth which is really *amātrā* or the mora-less part which is represented by the point (*bindu*) of the *anusvara*. The phases of the Self are *Viśva, Taijasa, Prājña* and the *Turīya;* the first three stand for the Self in

waking, dream and sleep respectively, and the
fourth is the Self *per se*. The principle of the
meditation on *Om* is to equate the *mātrās* with
the phases. Gaudapada calls the knowledge
or equation *mātrāsampratipatti,* (*i.e.,* knowing
the *mātrās* to be identical with the phases)
and *omkārasyapādaśovidyā* (knowledge of the
morae of *Om* as the phases of the Self). Now,
if two things are to be identified or compared
there must be some similarity between them.
Mandukya and, following it, the Karika,
give reasons in each case for the identification
of the phases of the Self with the *mātrās*. And
the reasons, it is advisable to remember, are
intended only for helping concentration on the
significance of *Om*.

The first of the *mātrās* is *a* and the first of
the phases is *Viśva*. These two are to be
regarded as identical because of the common
quality of being the first (*ādi*) as well as that
of pervading (*āpti*). Of the sound components of *Om*, *a* is the first; so also of the
aspects of the Self, *Viśva* is the first. And
just as *a* is pervasive of all speech, *Viśva* is
pervasive of the universe. In the case of the
second *mātrā u,* and the second phase of the
Self, *Taijasa*, the common qualities are exalta-

tion (*utkarṣa*) and intermediateness(*ubhayatva*).
The exaltation of *u* is due to its being·subsequ-
ent to *a*. Similarly *Taijasa* is exalted over *Viśva*
because of its superior order. *U* is intermediate
between *a* and *m*; and *Taijasa* is between *Viśva*
and *Prājña*. The common features that constitute the basis for the identification of *m* and
Prājña are being the measure(*miti* or *māna*) and
the locus of mergence (*apiti* or *laya*). In repeating *Oṁ* again and again, *a* and *u* merge into
and emerge from *m,* as it were. Here *ṁ* is
said to be the measure of the other two *mātrās*.
Prājña is the measure of *Viśva* and *Taijasa*
because these two evolve out of it in creation
and enter into it in dissolution; the worlds of
waking and dream get resolved in sleep, and
from sleep they emerge again. The second
common quality is *laya* or disappearance;
just as *a* and *u* end in *m*, *Viśva* and *Taijasa*
disappear in *Prājña*. It will be clear that the
letters *a*, *u* and *m* are employed in this meditation as mnemonics. Each letter stands for the
first letter of the wordssignifying certain features
of the Self in its manifestation as *Viśva, Taijasa*
and *Prājña*. The second quality of *Prājña*
is the only exception. Thus *a* stands for *ādi*
and *āpti;* *u* for *utkarṣa* and *ubhayatva;* and *m*
for *miti* or *māna*.

The fourth *mātrā* is, as we said already, *amātrā*. It is the silence into which the sound *Om* culminates. It is the *Om* without the distinction of parts. It has not even a name, and therefore it does not come under the purview of empirical usage. It is the *Turiya,* Self or Pure Consciousness which transcends the distinctions involved in the forms of *Viśva* and *Taijasa*, and the seed of plurality implicit in *Prājña*.

The Mandukya-upanishad eulogizes the meditation on the identity of the *mātrās* and the phases of the Self by specifying the fruit which each stage in the meditaton yields. He who knows Vaisavnara, (*i.e., Viśva*) as *a,* says the Upanishad, obtains all desires and becomes first among the great. He who knows the identity of *Taijasa* with *u* exalts or increases the continuity of knowledge and becomes equal or of the same attitude towards all and in his family none who does not know *Brahman* is born. He who knows the one-ness of *Prājña* and *ṁ* measures the whole world,(*i.e.,* knows its true nature) and becomes the place of its mergence, (*i.e.,* he becomes the Self which is the cause of the universe). He who knows the mora-less *Oṁkāra* in its fullness as signifying the *Turiya* realizes the Self and does not return to empirical life.

Meditation or *upāsanā* is defined thus by Sankara: the process of taking hold of some stay or *ālambana*, established as such in the sacred texts, and directing a continuous flow of even modes of the mind towards it, without the intervention of any other cognition contrary to it, is *upāsanā*. There must be some point of attention for concentration. This is the *ālambana* (support). It is of service in steadying the thought-current and making it flow in one direction. The *pratīkas* or images are useful in this way. The centrifugal tendency of the mind is arrested, and it becomes unflickering and one pointed like the flame of a lamp kept in a still place. The images which are wrongly called idols have á place in spiritual discipline because they help to direct the mind of the aspirant Godward.

That *Praṇava* or *Omkāra* has the pride of place among the symbols of the invisible Spirit, we have already stated. Its significance and the method of meditation thereon have also been explained. Gaudapada concludes his exposition of *Praṇava-yoga* by praising it and those who

practise it. "The mind should be yoked to
Praṇava, for *Praṇava* is *Brahman* in which
there is no fear. For him who is ever identified
with *Praṇava* there is no fear anywhere. *Praṇava*
is the lower *Brahman;* it is the higher also. It
has no cause; there is nothing besides it, nothing
outside it. Nor is there anything that follows
from it. *Praṇava* is immutable. It is the
beginning, the middle and the end of all. He
who knows *Praṇava* thus attains the Self.
Om is to be known as the Lord present in the
heart of all. Having understood the all-
pervading *Om,* the wise one does not grieve
about anything. *Omkāra* is without measure
(*amātrā*), and is without limits (*ananta-mātrā*);
It is That in which all duality ceases, It is bliss.
He who knows this is a saint, and no other."

—O—

MEDITATION ACCORDING TO ASHTANGA-YOGA

by

SWAMI VIJNANANDA

Man is ever in search of peace and happiness; but real and perennial peace and bliss are to be found in one's self alone and not in the sensate objects of pleasure. Our self is of the nature of pure being, consciousness and bliss. It is our essential nature; but the self is enveloped by ignorance, by the sheaths of body and mind, by our worldly passions, desires and activities. One has to practise yoga in order to pierce through these psychic strata and reach one's self. Absolute control and sublimation of mental states is the only way to become aware of the self. This control and, sublimation are brought about by Abhyasa, Vairagya and meditation.

Abhyasa means continued effort to steady the mind and Vairagya or non-attachment means self-mastery obtained by giving up all desires. Non-attachment brings about tran-

quillity of mind. With a tranquil mind, concentration and meditation become easy. Meditation with a concentrated mind illumines the
self. Meditation is an integral part of spiritual
life. It is a direct means to spiritual enlightenment. When a man takes to meditation, he
takes the path that leads directly to deliverance.

Meditation is an important limb of
Ashtanga-yoga. Ashtanga-yoga is not a
science of enquiry (pariksha-sastra); but is a
science of instruction (upadesa-sastra). So,
it is more practical than speculative in its
intent and content. It is not based on mere
theory or hypothesis; but on facts that have
been tested and proved. Ashtanga-yoga is a
practical mode of discipline in which the
self achieves independence and liberation. It
is not concerned with problems of philosophy. Neither is it burdened with logical
intricacies. Its only interest lies in helping
man to free himself from ignorance, from
bondage of body and mind, from the stress
and strain of life and to achieve peace and
happiness.

The key-word in Ashtanga-yoga is the
term yoga. Though the word 'yoga' may
mean several things, it specially and specifi-

cally means meditation in Ashtanga-yoga. Through meditation the self or the soul becomes liberated from the shackles of the mechanism of the body and mind. Mind is less binding than the gross body. Like the body it is also a form of matter. The goal of yoga is to completely extricate the spirit from every vestige of matter, be it body or mind.

Man in his essential nature is not the complex of body and mind. He is a spirit inhabiting a body. He has forgotten his spiritual nature. Due to ignorance, he identifies himself with the body and mind. As a result, he feels miserable and wretched. He is suffering from conflicts and is not at peace either with himself or with the world. By means of meditation man realises his true nature and remains in it. His ties with the body and mind become severed and he attains to serene peace and unalloyed bliss.

There are five obstacles to yoga. They are ignorance (avidya), self-consciousness (asmita), attachment (raga), aversion (dvesha) and desire to cling to life (abhinivesa). To consider what is non-eternal as eternal, what is impure as pure, what is painful as pleasant, etc.,

'7

is ignorance. Ignorance is the basic obstacle
from which all the other obstacles stem forth.
Erroneous identification of the self with the
body and mind is self-consciousness. Attachment means that which makes a man dwell
upon what is pleasurable and aversion means
that which makes a man dwell on what is
painful. The instinctive desire to cling to life
and dread of death constitute what is called
abhinivesa.

Since the self is enveloped by the sheaths of
body and mind, impurities pertaining to them
are to be eliminated before one can have a
vision of the self. Patanjali prescribes Ashtanga-yoga, *i.e.,* yoga consisting of eight
limbs for the purification of the mechanism
of the body and mind and for gaining a direct
vision of the self. The eight limbs are yama,
niyama, asana, pranayama, pratyahara,
dharana, dhyana and samadhi. The first five
are the external limbs while the latter three
are internal.

The first two, yama and niyama are meant
to chasten and direct our will in the right
direction. Cultivation of these two is very
necessary for higher life because they together

constitute the moral foundation upon which the whole of spiritual sadhana is based. Without these two, no spiritual sadhana becomes effective.

Yama comprises five virtues; ahimsa, satya, asteya, brahmacharya and aparigraha. Ahimsa means abstaining from harming others in any way at any time. It virtually means renunciation of hatred towards all beings. A spiritual sadhaka should not injure any being either by word, deed or thought. This becomes possible by the cultivation of (a) maitri or friendliness towards those who are happy (b) karuna or compassion towards those who are unhappy, (c) delight in the company of the virtuous people and (d) indifference towards the wicked.

Satya means speech and mind corresponding to the reality of things. It should be cultivated for the good and happiness of all and not for hurting the feelings of anybody. Satya ceases to be so if anybody is hurt by it. An aspirant should not indulge in falsehood or unnecessary talk.

Asteya means abstaining from appropriating things not sanctioned by the sastras or belong-

ing to others. Brahmacharya is sex-purity
in thought, word and deed. It is the most
essential virtue in spiritual life. Aparigraha
consists in non-acquisition of things. An
aspirant has to possess only as much as is
necessary to keep his body and mind in a fit
condition to carry on spiritual practice without being hindered by hunger or disease.

These categorical imperatives are to be
observed under all circumstances irrespective
of time, place and exigency.

Next come the disciplines collectively called
niyamas.   They are saucha, santòsha, tapas,
svadhyaya and Iswarapranidhana.

Saucha means physical cleanliness and mental
purity.   Regular bath keeps the body clean and
remembrance of God makes the mind pure.
Santosha or contentment consists in being
satisfied and happy with what one gets by due
exertion and in not coveting more.   Tapas or
austerity does not consist in unnecessarily
violating one's body or mind.   It consists more
in bearing the pairs of opposites like heat and
cold, pain and pleasure, etc., with equanimity
than in self-infliction. Svadhyaya consists in
the study of scriptures that are conducive to

one's liberation. Iswarapranidhana or devotion to God consists in offering oneself and one's actions to the Supreme Teacher.

Now we come to the next limb of yoga called asana or posture. An easy and steady posture which will enable the sadhaka to practise meditation without feeling any mental strain or physical discomfort and at the same time which will not lull the mind to sleep is to be adopted. A steady posture with limbs of the body remaining restful is *sine qua non* for meditation. If the posture is unsteady and limbs are restless, the mind and the senses also become restless and unmanageable. It is a matter of common experience that concentration and contemplation become easy and smooth when sitting in a steady and easy posture. Asana is an aid to mental equilibrium and poise. When asana is perfected fickleness of mind ceases. That asana which is steady and pleasant is considered to be the most suitable.

Then comes pranayama, the control of breath. Pranayama helps in restraining and regulating breath. Breathing and mind are closely connected. Whenever the mind is disturbed, the

breathing becomes irregular. Rhythmic breathing calms down the mind. Prana on the
physical plane appears as breathing which on
the subtle plane is connected with the functioning of mind. By controlling prana on the
physical plane the waves of the mind are
controlled. This is pranayama. It is said in the
Patañjali yoga-sastra that pranayama destroys
the ignorance caused by our past karma. It
must be noted that though pranayama is an
integral limb of yoga, it is, according to Patañjali,
a psycho-somatic means for a spiritual end.
When pranayama is practised under the super-
vision of a competent teacher, it conduces to
good health; but when practised haphazardly
and unscientifically, it is very likely to produce
mental and physical disorders. So, one has to
practise it with great care.

The next step in Ashtanga-yoga is pratyahara, *i.e.,* withdrawing the sense-organs from
sense-objects with the help of the mind. The
sense-organs obey and follow the mind. If
the mind is self-controlled, it can easily control
the sense-organs and withdraw them from the
sense-objects.

Now we come to dharana. It consists in

fixing the mind on an object. The object may
be internal like a lotus imagined in the heart
or may be external like the flame of a lamp.
The mind is accustomed to wander about;
so, it is not easy to fix the mind on an object
internal or external. Repeatedly, the mind
strays away from the object. But by repeated practice and perseverance and by cultivation of detachment, the mind can be made to
stick to an object.

Dharana matures into dhyana or meditation. Meditation consists in an unbroken flow
of thought towards the object of concentration. In meditation, the mind remains fixed
for a while on the object of concentration.
It is like pouring of oil from one vessel to another
in a steady uninterrupted flow. In the process
of meditation a succession of similar thoughts
flow in the mind without any contrary or
dissimilar thoughts interfering in the middle.

When meditation becomes continuous and
constant, mind takes the form of the object
of meditation itself. This state is called
samadhi. This is the culminating stage of
Ashtanga-yoga. In this state the self becomes
liberated from its conditioned existence. This

samadhi is called samprajnata samadhi because
there is consciousness of object in this samadhi.
There is another samadhi called asamprajnata
samadhi or objectless samadhi. In this there
is no consciousness of object; but it is not
void because there is pure consciousness in it.
This state is also known as nirvikalpa samadhi.
In this state, a yogi remains in his real nature.
It is a state of supreme peace and bliss.

The object or chosen ideal of meditation
could be impersonal or could be personal *i.e.,*
a person invested with holiness and divinity.
Meditation on the impersonal is rather difficult. The mind cannot operate except through
name and form. Any symbol of God or form
of God which appeals to the heart of the
sadhaka would be the ideal object for meditation. The object or chosen ideal may be
imagined to be seated in the lotus of the heart.

There are many impediments to meditation
like physical ailments, mental lassitude, doubt
as to the utility of meditation, sense-attractions,
non-attainment of concentration, etc. These
must be warded off. Moderation in food, sleep,
activity, wakefulness, etc., is also essential.
Exciting foods should be eschewed.

A simple and sure faith in God and a total dependence on His grace help in making meditation and spiritual life easy and smooth. Meditation becomes all the more smooth and joyous when there is love for God.

Meditation serves two purposes. By means of meditation the sadhaka devotes himself to his chosen ideal; secondly, by means of meditation the sadhaka becomes able to penetrate to the core of the Reality. As many people seem to think, meditation is not a process of discursive reasoning. It is a means of concentration by which the sadhaka seeks to elevate his consciousness. By means of regular practice of meditation, the sadhaka becomes able to gain more and more concentration and to approximate more and more closely to the ideal of perfection. If the meditation is well established in the sadhaka, it ceases to be mere meditation. It acquires the character of perception. The object or the chosen ideal of meditation becomes the object of perception. This state, called samadhi, liberates the soul from the meshes of the body and the mind. It is a state of infinite joy and supreme peace that passeth understanding.

There is no need even for those who have
no faith in dogmatic religion to despair of the
conflicts and complexities of their life. They
need not feel that their lives are in vain and
devoid of any meaning. Yoga and meditation
help men to solve their problems of life and
to make their lives meaningful, purposeful
and peaceful. Meditation is a real science
and so it is universal. Anybody, whether
believing in God or not, whether of the orient
or of the occident, can study it and practise it.

Integration of personality is the panacea
for all of our ills of life. Meditation helps to
bring about this integration of personality.
It is well known that man has the three faculties
of thought, will and feeling. When these are
at variance with each other we feel disturbed
in mind and suffer from conflicts. But when
thought, will and feeling act in unison, we
feel at peace with ourselves. So, thought,
will and feeling are to be co-ordinated with
each other and made to work in a spirit of
harmony if we are to feel at ease and happy.
Aberrations of thought, will and feeling are
responsible for the lack of harmony and for the
consequent disintegration of personality. So,
these aberrations are to be consciously rectified

and the whole mind should be harmoniously unified if integration of personality is to take place. Meditation helps us to correct the wayward vagaries and aberrations of thought, will and feeling and to purify, to unify and to harmonise our mind and thus to bring about integration by directing our thought, will and feeling towards our chosen ideal of meditation. Also, meditation gives a higher orientation to our thought, will and feeling; and exalts them.

Meditation is a manifold blessing. Man suffers from so many fears and frustrations. Swami Vivekananda says that ignorance of our spiritual nature, Atman, is the root cause of all our fears and frustrations. Ignorance creates a feeling of inherent weakness in man. Atman is the embodiment of strength. So, the best way of getting rid of our fears and frustrations is to know and feel our spiritual nature, the Atman. The purpose of yoga and meditation is to help us to discover and realise our true nature, the Atman and thus to rid ourselves of all our fears and frustrations.

—O—

MEDITATION IN CHRISTIANITY

Swami Nityabodhananda

The Hindu and Jewish-Christian traditions grew up on different soils and in different spiritual climates. Nevertheless, common points like union with the God-head or God in the impersonal and personal aspects as the goal of human destiny and ways to the goal such as meditation and prayer make our study of absorbing interest.

The term 'meditation' is used a few times in the Psalms of the old Testament.

"How much I love Thy Law
It is the object of my meditation."

(Psalm 119, 97)

"O Eternal, I meditate on your works."

(Psalm 143, 5)

Invoking the *name* of the Eternal is also mentioned in the old Testament:

"He (the Eternal) is always close to us whenever we invoke
His name."

(Deuteronomy II. 4, 7.)

In the New Testament the terms prayer, worship and contemplation bring together the various shades of meaning that Yoga-Vedanta gives to the term meditation. And when we say this, meditation should be understood both as act and attitude.

In St. John IV. 22, Jesus says, "God is Spirit; they that worship Him must worship Him as Spirit."

When the spirit is mentioned for the second time, it denotes the attitude of the worshipper. Only when the worshipper spiritualises himself, can God be worshipped as Spirit which reminds the Hindu of the Hindu dictum "*devo bhūtvā devam yajet*" To worship God one should become God, as pure as God. The various purifications or *śuddhis* are implied.

Prayer figures greatly as effective means to union with God with the early pillars of Christianity like St. Augustine. But more systematic meditation-material comes to us with mystics like St. John of the Cross and St. Theresa of Avila. St. John of the Cross speaks of the four 'Nights' as four purifications necessary for the final mystical union and also of the ten steps of the Ladder of Perfection. This we

shall consider later on. Then comes the
Philokalia tradition with detailed instructions
of prayer-meditation on the heart, so that the
heart absorbs the Lord and the Lord the heart.
With these preliminary remarks we can proceed
further.

Jesus and prayer-meditation

Luke XI, suggests that there was evidence
in Jesus's praying of an unusual closeness to
God. Jesus prayed alone and sometimes prayed
the whole night. 'Alone' may mean in
solitude as is evidenced in the instructions Jesus
gave: "When you pray, enter into thy closet
and when thou hast shut thy door, pray to thy
Father which is in secret, and the Father which
seeth in secret, shall reward thee openly.'
(Matthew VI-6). The insistence on 'secret'
may be understood as the secret depth of the
heart where one has to retire and into which
depth God sees.

In the Lord's prayer, which Jesus bequeathed
to humanity, there is the power of realizing the
Kingdom in the present moment of prayer
as also of the daily spiritual sustenance, faith
hope and love, symbolized by the daily bread.

Testimony of the Disciples

John I. 14 says "We contemplated his (Jesus's) glory, full of Grace, and Truth." This contemplation-meditation should be understood as an echo of the contemplation to which Jesus himself refers when he says: "God is spirit and those who want to contemplate Him in truth should do so in spirit."

The result of this contemplation or communion with him is the acquisition of Light. In his first epistle John says: "If we say that we have communion with Him and walk in darkness, we lie. But if we walk in the light as He is in the Light, we have communion with Him and one with another......"
(1 John, 6, 7).

St. Francis of Assisi (1182-1226)

St. Francis of Assisi, the tallest tower of mediaeval Christian mysticism has left behind a great treasure of his prayers and meditations. What he speaks of his vision of two lights a few days before receiving the stigmata, may help in our meditation too. To his close associate Brother Leon he says:

"During that prayer two lights were shown to me: one in which I recognized God; and the other in which I recognized myself. And when I asked God who I was in comparison with Him, I plunged deep in contemplation where I felt the infinite depth of God's bounty as also the sad abyss of my spiritual misery."

So long as St. Francis saw the two 'lights', peace did not descend into him. When the light in which he saw himself as creature disappeared and became one with the Divine light the night before he received the stigmata, then only complete union with Christ became a living reality.

The prayer he has transmitted to us is absolutely inspiring at all moments:

"O Lord make me an instrument of your
    Peace:
        so that
            Where there is hatred,
                I can bring love
            Where there is offence,
                I can bring pardon
            Where there is discord,
                I bring union
            Where there is error,
                I bring truth

> Where there is doubt,
>   I bring faith
> Where there is despair,
>   I bring hope
> Where there is darkness,
>   I bring light
> Where there is sorrow,
>   I bring joy.

Meister Eckhart (early 14th Century)

Meister Eckhart, called a scholastic mystique rather than a mystical scholastic, offered us very Advaitic meditations. For him the experience of 'purely existing' that we have in self-identity is the highest where Pure Being and experience of God mix and mingle. "In that unconditioned Being which is above God I was myself and what I am now, I knew myself. Therefore I am my first cause and in it all things were born. I am at the same time my eternal being and temporal being. It is to realize this immortal birth that I am born. I shall never die, I am the cause of all things." All this reminds us of the '*Aham Brahmāsmi*' (I am Brahman) of the Upanishads.

Meditations of St. John of the Cross

St. John of the Cross (1542-1591) was pre-

eminently a Bhakti-yogin. His Ishtam was
Jesus Christ and his relationship with the
Ishtam was that of *mādhyurya*, that of the
Gopis with Sri Krishna; St. John was the bride
thirsting for union with his beloved Christ.

He practised and taught four stages of
purification to come to that union, stages
which he called in a special sense 'Nights'.
When the lights that guide human understanding and love are extinguished, God's
light enters into man. This is a blinding light
and a blinding day. But what is night for the
unregenerate man is day for the regenerate.

The first meditation is on the purification
of the senses by withdrawal from their objects
and by a godward turn given to them. "The
appetite is the mouth of the will' and when
the appetite of the senses is nourished by
Sattvic food, then the will becomes Sattvic
and pure and by a pure will constant remembrance of God is easily acquired.

This meditation of St. John compares well
with the *pratyāhāra* which is the fifth step in
the ladder of Patanjali's eight-step yoga. The
withdrawal of the organs from their objects by

the conviction that all forms are in the mind, is
Pratyāhāra.

The second Sanjuaniste meditation is on the
purification of understanding through faith.
Clarifying the notion the mystic doctor says:
'In this stage the soul remains for long hours
lost in oblivion, beyond time and united with
celestial intelligence. The soul feels the savour
of love without knowing what it loves in particular, a general amorous knowledge. God at
this stage plunges us in obscure faith. Faith
at this stage cannot be analyzed or known by
our superior intelligence, not even by the faculty
that distinguishes between being and non-being.
From henceforth faith becomes the light and
guide of our soul. St. John says that at this
stage the soul acquires the resemblance of God
(*sādharmya*).

The third meditation is on the purification
of memory by hope, the hope of salvation.
We are all so deeply attached to our personal
memories and this attachment shuts off the
memory which God has placed in us, the
memory of His free Nature, Salvation.

In the language of the Gita cleansing of
memory by Grace is gaining recognition of the

true nature of the Self and loosening all the ties of the heart.   (Gita, XVIII. 73).

The fourth meditation according to St. John of the Cross is purification of the will by love, the night of the will by love. The act of loving God is an act of will, an openness of will. It is neither emotion nor intellect that is involved in this act. To love by sentiment is shallow; to love by emotion leads us to feebleness and to emotionalism. To love by intellect is dry. But to love by the will to live and to love, which God has placed in us, is to pour out our whole being into God and be transformed into His being (*Ātmasamarpaṇa*).

When the momentum to love God comes from the will then of the two wills, of man's and of God's, there will be only one. In order to gain this momentum the will must be cleansed of joy, hope, pain and fear.

The Ladder of Perfection

The first step is a kind of languor of love. Having lost all taste for the things of the world the soul finds neither help nor taste nor comfort nor rest in anything. Renunciation of all gratification of the senses, memory and imagination is the second and third step. The agonizing pain of separation is the fourth step. The fifth is a very high state of impatient union. This state of intense passionate love of excruciating agony of the soul is expressed in the first stanza of the 'Song of Songs'. The sixth step is the joy of betrothal, the first stage of equality of love with God. The seventh prolongs that state of union. The intense love makes him climb the eighth step. The ninth step is for St. John the perfect state. The Holy Spirit infuses in the aspirant a supreme love of sweetness and bliss. This state quickly leads the soul to the tenth degree of the ladder wherein the soul experiences total union with God and the saint adds at this stage that the soul is ready to leave the body: the soul is God 'by participation'. It is a stage of 'clear vision' wherein the soul is totally assimilated with God. The ten steps show complimentarity with the stages through which the mystic soul passes through as indicated in St. Theresa's writings: (1) Prayer of quiet, (2) Prayer of full union, (3) Prayer of Ecstasy, (4) Prayer of transforming union. St. Theresa was a contemporary of St. John of the Cross.

The Philokalia Meditation

The Philokalia is a collection of writings of the Fathers from the earliest times after the Declaration of Constantine the Great. The word 'Philokalia' means love of the beautiful, the exalted, the good. More precisely it contains an interpretation of the secret life in Lord Jesus Christ (which is the truly Christian life, that develops and rises to perfection through prayer of the heart.

'A true sanctuary is a heart free from thoughts, made active by the Spirit. For there all is said and done spiritually' (*Philokalia*, p. 38). 'Plunging thought into light, so that thought itself becomes light, the mind guided by the Spirit traces words in the pure hearts of those who listen. Then it understands the words: "And they shall be all taught of God" (John VI, 45)' (*Philokalia p.* 42).

What is the prayer used by the tradition? "Lord Jesus Christ, Son of God, have mercy upon me!"

"If one, instead of all other thoughts, forces to have only this one constant prayer within, if one continues to do this with one's whole

attention, then in time it will open for him the
way to the heart." (*Philokalia,* p. 34).

How to practise prayer

"In the morning force your mind to descend from the head to the heart and hold it
there, calling ceaselessly in mind and soul:
'Lord Jesus Christ, have mercy upon me.'
Let the memory of Jesus combine with your
breath—then will you know the profit of
silence" (Ibid. p. 85).

"The beginning of every action pleasing to
God is calling with faith on the life-saving
name of our Lord Christ, as He Himself said:
'Without Me ye can do nothing' (John
XV, 5), together with 'the peace and love
which accompany this calling'" (Ibid. p. 194).

"In quality, prayer is communion (co-exist-
ence, merging into one being) and union
of man with God. In action, it is what the
world stands by, reconciliation with God,
the mother of tears and again their daughter,
propitiation for sin, a bridge over tempta-
tions, a wall against sorrows...." (Ibid.
p. 201).

Students of Yoga-Vedanta are quite conversant with its teaching that celebrates the importance of the heart in spiritual practices. The term in Sanskrit for heart is *hṛdayam* which literally means 'where the Lord resides.'

To Arjuna's question: "How shall I, ever meditating, know Thee, O Yogin, in what several aspects art Thou to be thought of by me?" (Gita X, 17) the Lord replies: "I am the Self, O Gudakesa, seated in the heart of all beings.." (Gita X, 20).

Sri Sankara in his commentary on the verse says: "You should think of Me as the innermost self, seated in the heart within of all beings. He who is unable to think of Me as the Self should think of Me in those things which are mentioned in the Vibhuti Yoga of the 10th chapter of the Gita."

---

(1) "He that heareth my word and believeth in Him that sent me *hath* ever-lasting life." (John V. 24). The accent is on *hath* and not wilt have. Hearing is not simply with the ears but with the heart.

MEDITATION ACCORDING
TO SPANISH MYSTICS

The most outstanding figures among the
Spanish mystics are St. Theresa of Jesus
and St. John of the Cross. They were con-
temporaries and lived in the sixteenth century. Both of them belonged to the Carme-
lite Order and were instrumental in the ton-
ing up of and reforming the Order to which
they belonged and which was then in a dec-
lining state. St. Theresa also founded six-
teen convents and fourteen monasteries and
in her position as directress of a large number of novitiates had to constantly write letters
to guide them in their spiritual path. These
letters along with an autobiography which the
saint was asked to write by her confessors, have
been published in book-form.

St. John of the Cross was a well-learned
person who has left behind some beautiful
verses depicting the spiritual ascent of the
soul and its union with God. Explaining

the significance of these verses he has written a long commentary which has served as
a source of inspiration and guidance to the
earnest seekers of the Christian community
during the last two centuries.

When one goes through these works one
rarely comes across the word "meditation"
and when it occurs it is used in the sense of
imagination, ideation or phantasy.[1] Yet, its
usefulness and efficacy as a preparatory stage,
are not deprecated or discarded. However, the
Spanish mystics speak much of mental prayer
and contemplation, as means to union with God,
which may be, for all practical purposes, inter-
preted as meditation as we understand the
word nowadays. For example, to St. Theresa
prayer is not simply a mere utterance of some
words but an intimate conversation with the
Beloved. In a letter to the nuns she says:
"Try to think and understand, my children
with whom you are talking or going to talk.
Even in a thousand lives of ours we shall not
be able to know in what way the Lord deserves
to be treated, this Lord in whose presence even
the angels tremble. Everything is subject to
Him, He can do anything and His mere wish
is action. It is reasonable that we take de-

light in His grandeurs and be aware to whom
we are espoused and what grand life will be
ours."[2] Here she compares the Lord to a
beloved husband and says that one who has
taken up the spiritual path is already married
to Him. Then she places before the nuns the
duties of a truly devoted wife in the world and
how their own life and thoughts should be:
"In this world when a woman marries, she
knows to whom, his status in life and what he is.
Now, my children, we who are already married
to Him before the formal ceremony and are to
be taken to His abode, shall we not think of
Him? Those who are married to men here
do not discard these thoughts. Why then,
should we not try to know who this person is,
who his father, what is that land where he will
take us, what are the riches that he promises to
give and so on? Also, in what way shall we
be able to please him and in what way we
shall transform our state to conform with
that of his? In the world, a woman, who
desires to be devoted to her husband, is not
required to know everything else than these
things even if the husband be a very low
person. Should we then give lesser importance to our Lord than they do to men?
Further, if the husband is of a jealous nature

and wishes that the wife have no contact with
anyone, it will be strange indeed that she
should not think how best to satisfy him in this
respect, for in him are all the things that one
could desire! To know and understand these
truths is mental prayer."[3]

As we know, it is extremely difficult to concentrate on any particular subject for a long
time unless we have a keen interest in it. And
interest or taste for a thing unfolds itself only
when we find ourselves involved in, feel an
intimate relationship with, or affinity to, the
subject. In the spiritual world too this theory
or rule applies; so in thinking of God or meditating on Him, one has to establish a certain
relationship with Him, if one has to make
rapid progress. The mental prayer, as described above by St. Theresa, for the reason
just mentioned, can be termed as a type of
meditation. It helps the individual to dive deep
into the mystery of the divine relationship
and be aware of the benefit he receives in
developing such an attitude of mind. The
natural bent of the human mind is to seek a
return for whatever one does, even a philan-
thropist is moved to act by some hidden motive,
for example by a desire for name and fame. So

unless man gets convinced that the sacrifice he is going to make, by discarding the things of the world and giving up even the appetite for them, will bring him in the long run, immense benefit, he will not take to spiritual life in the real sense of the term. Hence arises the necessity for deep reflection over the lasting gain that one gets from one's constant contact with God. The purpose of the mental prayer cited above is to maintain one's mind continually on God which is also what meditation signifies. For this reason it may not be an error to call such a kind of prayer as meditation.

There is another form of prayer practised, in almost all religions, viz. vocal prayer. The Christians have a prayer which begins with the words: "Our Father who are in Heaven" and so on taught by Jesus himself. Advising the nuns as to how one should practise this prayer St. Theresa says: "The Master taught us by setting an example that this prayer be repeated in solitude, although it was not necessary for him. From this it is be understood that it is not possible to talk with God and the world at the same time, i.e., praying to God and simultaneously listening to what is being talked about or to think of things of the world, though sometimes and in some cases this latter cannot be avoided because of the infirmity of the body or illness. Others should try to be alone when they pray, so that they could be aware with whom they are and what response the Lord has to their prayers. Do you think that He is silent because we do not hear Him? Well does He respond to the heart when we ask from the bottom of our heart. And it is of much benefit that we should consider that it is to each one of us individually that the Lord teaches this prayer and that the teacher is never so far from the disciple as to necessitate the latter to call him aloud, rather he is always very near to the disciple. For this reason my advice to you is that it is good for you that you repeat this prayer of the Lord in a proper manner and with diligence.

"You will say that this type of praying amounts to reflection or meditation, and that you are not able to do it or do not want to do it, but to pray vocally: because you have little patience and are ill disposed to take any trouble, which latter are necessary in the beginning, for the withdrawal of the mind. You are right if you stipulate that the above form of praying amounts to mental prayer, but I certainly do not known how you can separate the vocal prayer from the mental, if the former is to be practised well, knowing or being conscious with whom we are talking."[4] She adds that one should try to pray with caution and with the introspection cited above as not to end in something superficial and unhelpful. "I have proved it," she continues, "and found that the best way is to try to have the thoughts directed towards Him to whom the words are addressed."[5]

Here we find that even while practising vocal prayer, the Spanish mystics exhort that it should be done in solitude and with the mind turned towards God. Such a prayer well done, they say, dulls all the outgoing tendencies or faculties of the mind such as understanding, memory and will. That is to say the intellect refrains from seeking to understand the external objects, the memory desists from bringing to the surface of the mind thoughts that would divert its attention from the main purpose or object in view, i.e. God, and the will abstains from wanting to do anything that contradicts or affects adversely the spiritual life of the individual.

"The self then understands that the Divine

Master is teaching it without having recourse
to words, suspending the functioning of the
faculties of the mind. For if these latter were
to be active they will do more harm than good.
Then they enjoy without understanding how;
the soul is enwrapt in love, but does not know
how it loves; knows that it enjoys what it loves
but does not understand how it enjoys. Well
does it understand that it is not that kind of
enjoyment that the common or ordinary
intellect conceives; and, the will merges in the
soul without knowing how, but at the same
time able to perceive that this good is not
something that could be achieved by all the
efforts that one can do in this world. It is a
gift of the Lord of the world and the heaven.
This, my children, is perfect contemplation."[6]

To understand better what has preceded
and what is to follow it is necessary to know
some of the principal concepts of the Spanish
mystics. St. John of the Cross speaks of the
spiritual night as the immediate means for the
union of the soul with the Divine. The soul
has, according to them, three potencies of
faculties, viz., understanding, memory and will,
whose supernatural objectives are the three
theological virtues, faith, hope and charity or

love, respectively. These three virtues are the means by which the soul unites with God, each one creating a vacuum and darkness in its respective faculty: faith in understanding or intellect, hope in memory and charity or love in the will. The understanding is to be perfected in the darkness of faith, memory in the vacuum of hope and the will buried in the lack of all sensual love, to go towards God. When these faculties are perfected in the above-said manner, one can clearly perceive what a great necessity there is that the soul, to travel safely in this spiritual path, should pass through this dark night, leaning on these three virtues, which empty it of all the things of the world. For the soul can unite with God in this life neither through reasoning, nor by enjoyment, nor through imagination, nor through any other sense organ, but only through faith, hope and love. Faith tells us what we cannot understand by the intellect or reasoning, and even if the intellect comes to grasp the certainty of the things manifested through faith, it is not able to understand clearly, rather finds itself groping in darkness.

Hope of uniting with God, without doubt, empties and darkens all memory of things

of this world and the next, because hope is
always of something one does not have and
does not see. Charity empties the will of its
resolutions to gain or obtain all external objects;
it compels us to love God above all things,
which cannot be done except through severing
the love to these and directing it all to God.
Thus these three virtues put the soul in the
darkness and emptiness of all things of the world.
And this is the dark spiritual night referred
to above as the immediate means for union
with God—to be blind towards things of the
world, to renounce them totally.

Now we have seen what are vocal prayer,
mental prayer and contemplation according
to the Spanish mystics and how the first two
go side by side: to be practised simultaneously,
to be effective. The third one, contemplation,
is meant for a very few and is a gift from God.

How to practise vocal prayer is next dealt
with. First of all one should examine one's
conscience and do other purificatory acts.
"Then, my children," advises St. Theresa to
her nuns, "seek company, because you are
alone. What company is better than that of
the Master, who taught the prayer that you

are going to recite? Imagine that the Master is beside you and you will discover with what love and kindness He is teaching you. Be not without such a friend as long as you can. If you get habituated to bring Him near to you and He perceives that you do it with love and are trying to content Him then He will never fail you; certainly He will help you in all your efforts, He will be with you everywhere."[7]

The practice recommended here helps to put the mind in a state of concentration. Even an aspirant who is not able to discriminate or reason about theological problems is asked to cultivate this habit. For, to fix the mind on one subject for a long time is a difficult task and cannot be accomplished without years of hard practice. Admonishes St. Theresa her novitiates: "I do not ask you that you develop profound and intricate reflections about the Lord; do not ask you anything more than that you look at Him. What is it that impedes you to direct, even though it is for some moments if not more, your soul's eyes towards this Lord? Well can you look at things very ugly, and can you not look at the most beautiful thing that can be imagined? Your Lord, my children, never takes His compassionate eyes off you, even though you might have acted a thousand times vilely against Him. Is it then too much to ask that you take off your eyes from the external objects and direct them, some times at least, toward Him? Listen , He does not expect anything else from you, than this much."[8]

"Further, in the world they say that if a woman were to be considered as devoted to the husband, she should manifest sorrow in his sorrow, and happiness in his happiness, though in reality she may not feel so. Look, from what servileness you have been saved. But this sympathy the Lord truly shows towards us; He assumes the role of the servant and desires you to be the mistress, to serve you at your pleasure. If you are cheerful you will see Him in His glorious state of resurrection, majestic, handsome, victorious and cheerful, like one who, in a battle, has conquered a great kingdom which He desires to give you along with Himself. Is it then too much to expect of you that you look at Him, once in a way; Him who gives you so liberally?"[9] These, says the saint, should be one's thoughts while praying.

What is the prayer that helps the soul to

draw within itself? Jesus prayed: "Our Father that art in Heaven" and so on. Commenting on this St. Theresa asks: "Do you think that it is of little importance to know what is Heaven and where to seek your heavenly Father? I tell you that for dispersed minds it is most important to understand this, not only to believe in but try to know it through experience; because it is one of the things that influences the understanding and helps to withdraw the soul into itself. You know that God is everywhere, omnipresent. It is evident, they say, that wherever the king is, there his court is; similarly, where God is, is Heaven. No doubt, you can believe that where God is, there all grandeur is. St. Augustine says that he searched for God in many places and finally found Him within himself. Do you think it is of no consequence for one with a dispersed mind to know this truth and perceive that it is not necessary to go to Heaven to speak with the Eternal Father, or to be sumptuously feasted by Him; that it is not even necessary to speak aloud? In however low a voice one may speak He will certainly hear us, for He is very near; one does not require wings to go in search of Him. What one has to do is to retire into solitude and see Him within oneself; treat such a good Guest as one's own and not as a foreigner, and with great humility speak to Him as one's own father, relate to Him one's difficulties, and seek solutions for these, knowing well that one is not fit to be a child of His."[10]

This prayer, accompanied by such thoughts as above, though practised vocally, helps to control the mind within a short time and does much good. It is called gathering of thoughts because the soul withdraws all its faculties and enters into itself with the Beloved, God. "The Divine Master comes to it within a much shorter time than by any other method, and blesses it with silent prayer. There the mind absorbed in itself can think of Christ's Passion, imagine there His presence and not tire itself trying to seek Him on Mt. Calvary and so on. Those who could in this way shut themselves up in this small heaven of their soul, where dwells He who made it as also this earth, and accustom not to look at nor be where the senses would be distracted, should be sure that they are treading an excellent path and will not fail to drink the water of the fountain of life." They are like those who go by boat, which with a litle favourable wind reaches its destination in a few days.

Those who begin to practise thus have, so

to say, already put to sea; who, though they have not left the land for ever, do what they can to free themselves from it by gathering their senses into the mind, at least during those moments. If the gathering of the senses is real and genuine, one feels it clearly because of the transformation that occurs in oneself: the self seems to rise beyond this play of the world, to become aware of better times and feels like a person who enters a fort to defend himself from the adversaries. Further, by such a withdrawal they shut their eyes to the things of the world, i.e., these latter have no power of attraction for such a man. On the other hand his inner eyes open to the wonders of the self. Thus whoever treads this path, if his prayer is constant, will overcome the lure of the worldly objects, defeat the baser instincts of the body and strengthen his mind. And though in the beginning one cannot feel this change it being so slow as to be imperceptible, yet if one persists in one's effort, say the Spanish mystics, one would clearly feel, how the mind gains control over the senses. They may go out again but would not be able to do any harm as before, because they go out as prisoners on parole or obedient subjects, who return immediately they are called back. With the repeated gathering of the senses by this method of prayer, God pleases to dispose that the soul be in perfect contemplation or total absorption.

Let us conclude with an idea that the Spanish mystic placed before the novitiates to help them withdraw their minds into themselves: "Suppose within you there is a palace with immense riches, edifices of gold, inlaid with precious stones, in short, fit for such a Lord, and that you are responsible for its structure (indeed, there is no structure of such beauty as a pure soul, full of virtues, which shine like gems) and that in it dwells the great King, who has condescended to be your Father and seated on the precious throne of your heart. This may appear to be childish, but is necessary for us so that we may grasp firmly the fact that there is something in us more precious than all the precious things that we see in the world outside. Let us not presume that we are empty within. I consider it impossible that we could give ourselves up to the ephemeral things, if once we become conscious of the presence of such a Guest within, because we shall then see how paltry these things of the world are."

References

1. San Juan de la Cruz, Obras Completas Vol. II page 98. Pub: Editorial Calomino, La Plata, Argentina. 1945 Edition.
2. Obras de Santa Teresa de Jesus, page 431, published by Apostolado de la Prensa, S.A., Velazquez 28, Madrid. Spain. 1948 Edition.
3. Ibid. p. 431.
4. Ibid. p. 436
5. Ibid. p. 437
6. Ibid. p 438
7. Ibid. pp. 438-39
8. Ibid. p. 440
9. Ibid. pp. 440-41
10. Ibid. p. 447.
11. Ibid. pp. 449-450.

MEDITATION AND THE INTELLIGENT ASPIRANT

Swami Sasirananda

A young man comes rushing in for an immediate interview. Reason? His examination is closing in, he can't get his mind to his studies and wants to be taught meditation. An elderly official, just retired from government service and very much agitated, seeks instructions regarding meditation. The next time he appears after a long interval he is no more agitated. Effect of practising meditation? No. After two days he could get re-employed! Men and women, confronted by problems and sufferings—often self-created—distraught and desperate, wish to try 'meditation' as a possible and instant remedy for their ills—whether physical. mental, social or economic.

Meditation is surely in great demand today, as a panacea for a variety of ills and evils and so it is not surprising that there has been a mushroom growth of 'Yogis' or 'masters', organizations and courses catering to these customers; it is not surprising that it has also become a large-scale business, and export-oriented as well. Besides, the occult and romantic expectations from meditation have made it an attraction for the sophisticated and so-called educated even more than for others who are considered superstitious. Undoubtedly meditation and the Yogi have acquired a glamour and glitter, which makes it all the more essential to sift out and understand, as far as we can, what are the facts and what is right and correct.

*   *   *

What is meditation? What is its real goal and purpose? What constitutes its right and fruitful path?

"The greatest help to spiritual life is meditation. In meditation we divest ourselves of all material conditions and feel our divine nature. We do not depend upon any external help in meditation," says Swami Vivekananda, the master Yogi of modern times, whom his Guru Sri Ramakrishna used to term as a *Dhyāna-Siddha,* a past-master in meditation. At the very beginning of Patanjali's "Yoga-sutras", the basic traditional autho-

rity on the Yoga of Meditation, we find it
clearly stated: "Yoga is the stopping or
elimination of thought-waves. And then one
is established in one's own glorious, essential
nature." Elsewhere, meditation is explained
by other teachers as a continual thought-current
directed towards a particular worthy object,
and to the exclusion of all other thoughts.

From the above statements certain facts stand
out clearly:

i) Meditation is a very high state, border-
ing on the divine, if not actually so.

ii) Its main goal is not so much concentrating the mind on anything 'else'; not so
much acquisition of any object or state, however
covetable otherwise, external to oneself. It is
taking off all and every thought of the external,
to cease depending on the external, to come
back to one's own essential blissful core and
rest in it, free from any kind of dependence,
want, fear, doubt or discontent.

iii) All that the earnest aspirant should
aspire after, or all that is worth aspiring is
deep within oneself, an integral, inalienable
part of oneself. As such, all his effort should

be directed towards extricating the mind and its thoughts from getting involved in, and running after, the petty, transient external world, the 'non-self'. And then one should direct the mental energy thus mobilised, the thought-stream resulting from it, to one's inmost self where it will rest. Time and direct experience will reveal that this inmost self is the gateway to all that man really aspires after, to all that he really needs; it is the gateway to all the peace and happiness he eternally hankers after, to all the power, knowledge and joy that he seeks; it is the gateway to the seat of all the 'gods' he may be trying to propitiate or praying to—and to 'God', the Supreme Spirit, who is the highest object of the devotee's love and devotion.

*   *   *

What happens when one succeeds in meditation of the right kind is beautifully and succintly stated by the *Bhagavad-Gita*: "One rejoices in one's Self. One experiences that ultimate and pure happiness, which is beyond the range of the senses. Having gained that, one finds there is no greater gain to enquire after. Established therein, even the heaviest of sorrows are not able to shake him. This Yoga, in fact, takes one beyond even contact with pain. And

it is this Yoga (and 'meditation' or 'Dhyana'
which immediately leads to it) that is to be
practised with resolute enthusiasm."

An intelligent aspirant will always be able
to discriminate clearly and make out what is
the real goal of any Sadhana and what constitutes the proper means. The goal of true
meditation is the experience of complete freedom
or total independence which makes one deeply
calm and contented, of unalloyed inner bliss
which manifests as spontaneous love and service,
and an illumined understanding which elimina-
tes all doubt and fear. When one has attained
to these virtues, what else is he but 'divine'?
And all that works and helps towards this would
constitute the means.

So wealth or creature comforts, health or
longevity, powers of intellect or other talents,
enjoyments of the most intense pleasures and
even the possession of psychic powers—each
and all of them can never be the end in themselves; they cannot be the 'goal' one seeks in
Meditation. Rightly and discriminately used,
they may serve as temporary stepping stones
or passing 'mile-stones' on the path, at best.
But he who, forgetting the great and sublime
goal of freedom, independence and pure bliss,

seeks to make meditation a means to lesser ends is misguided, an object of pity. He is bound to end up in ultimate frustration, though for a brief while he may think that something wonderful has been achieved and for which others too may glorify him.

The genuine, wise aspirant will, therefore, never consciously seek the petty and passing things which the ignorant go after, will not encourage the presence of such seekings while meditating and will never offer prayer for such things. His seeking and prayers will be only for light, more light, for truth, higher truth and for real freedom which makes him rise above all limitations.

Worldly problems and situations have to be countered at their own appropriate level. Most often the remedies to our sufferings lie in a more intelligent understanding of the situation, avoidance of unhealthy habits and ways of life, and cultivation of healthy ones. But people fail to do what is to be done at the appropriate level and ignorantly seek easy and instant remedy through 'meditation' or 'prayer'.

*   *   *

Even the genuine aspirant has to realise
that meditation requires a reasonably healthy
body and nerves. And he will have to keep
them in constant good repair by proper control and care regarding his food, sleep, work
and recreation. Meditation requires the finest
and most powerful component of human
energy; it is not just a process of relaxing,
forgetting and retiring. Good, positive habits
are very essential and that not just for a day or
two, but over years and years, perhaps a
life-time.

As such the tendency to seek instant and
easy remedies and short-cuts to spiritual 'boons'
should be relentlessly eschewed. One should
constantly remember the wholesome advice
given by Patanjali: "Thoughts have to be
controlled by practice and non-attachment.
Practice means continuous struggle to keep the
thoughts restrained. And this practice becomes
firmly grounded only by long, constant and
enthusiastic effort." The key to success in
Sadhana is love and enthusiasm for the objective to be achieved as well as for the path to be
trodden, and not a grudging, strained and
impatient approach which is ever thinking
how soon all the bother would be over. There

is no holiday in spiritual life, no retirement.
Who would ever seek a holiday from that
which is after one's own heart? The right
aspirant, on the other hand, would feel bad
were he to be forced to take a holiday or retire
from it.

*   *   *

Among the many obstacles which one
encounters when taking to the path of meditation, not a few of them are the result of
either lack of the needed preliminary equipment and preparation or of wrong approaches.
In this context, it would be well to note specially
that in Patanjali's eight-stage scheme of Yoga,
meditation is the seventh stage, just before the
grand culmination of *samādhi,* and the aspirant
is naturally expected to have reasonable ground-
ing in the earlier six stages before reaching the
seventh.

Leaving aside the third and fourth stages
relating to posture and rhythmic breathing
(which because of their physical nature have
received attention out of proportion to their
importance in, and relevance to, the entire
Yoga scheme), one should pay special attention to the first and second, and fifth and sixth
stages. The first two steps dealing with ethical

virtues and inner purity are the very foundations
of Yoga—without which no worthwhile super-
structure can be built.   They lay down that one
who proceeds on the path of meditation should
be inclined, naturally or by practice, towards
truth, non-injury or kindness, non-acquisitiveness
or greedlessness, and chastity; to cleanliness,
contentment, readiness for an austere life of
striving, and a humble spirit of self-surrender
to God.

An assiduous practice of these virtues is
indispensable; for on the one hand their absence
makes right meditation impossible; on the
other, even if one does not take up meditation,
in themselves they are great assets for man to
succeed in any walk of life, sacred or secular.
When we bear this in mind, it becomes clear
how misleading and dangerous certain self-
styled teachers of Yoga can be when they either
play down, ignore or brazenly declare as unnecessary, the need for moral and ethical
purity.   One who is well-grounded in these
virtues classed under *yama* and *niyama* is
already halfway on the road to success; and perfection in them easily leads him on to *samādhi*
itself.   Such a one is bound to be a blessing
to oneself and to society.

The fifth and sixth stages, termed, *pratyā-hāra* and *dhāraṇā* are also very important for the aspirant. In fact, what most people try to do, when they are said to be 'meditating' can, at best, come only under these two heads. *Pratyāhāra* is the detaching and withdrawing of the senses from their external objects; it is the checking of mental energy from its dissipating outward movements. And *Dhāraṇā* is the focussing or concentrating of the mental or psychic energy thus saved on some worthy object. It will be obvious to any thinking person that if he is not reasonably grounded in the virtues of *yama* and *niyama,* he will not, or cannot, detach himself from the undesirable pulls of the external world, and as such not much energy will be available for concentration. And remember, only sustained and intense concentration of a high order can lead on to real 'meditation'.

Apart from the unfitness of the morally impure person to achieve any degree of meditation, even his efforts at concentration may lead to adverse results including strain, breakdown, and also undesirable social consequences.

Many of us freely mix and interchange the

terms 'concentration' and 'meditation'. In this
context, it may be noted that 'concentration'
of mind, again, is a means and not the end.
There is concentration and concentration, good
and bad. A person's thoughts, when subject
to lust or anger or greed, are concentrated
indeed. Many vicious persons and enemies
of society can have very concentrated minds.
It is those without moral purity, but with
power of concentration, who turn out to be
demons, our mythological *Rāvanas* and the like.
Even if one can concentrate the mind without
moral purification, the concentrated energy
will go to feed only the vices, as in an unweeded
garden most of the water and manure supplied
will go to nourish the weeds, useless or poisonous,
and the regular plants will remain starved or
smothered. So what is needed is concentration
with purity, never *without*.

Actually many of the complaints of those
who try to practise concentration and meditation arise from this direction, *viz.*, lack of
sufficient purity, of clean and healthy body
and nerves, of sense-control. Meditation as
such is not only no strain, but intensely refreshing and joy-generating. The strain one experiences in Sadhana is due to the downward pulls

caused by uncontrolled senses and wrong life-habits. The solution lies not in diluting or giving up 'meditation' but in having more and more personal purity, of control over senses and habits.

*   *   *   *

Even to aspirants, well qualified, certain doubts and difficulties present themselves. What is to be the object of concentration, whether a black dot or a candle-flame? 'within' or 'without'? and in which 'centre?' While some of the details and proper directions should be obtained only through personal communication with one's spiritual guide, some general observations would not be out of place. All 'objects' of concentration are only aids to concentration and not the goal. An inner object is better than an outer, and a living one better than a non-living. Best of all is a holy personality. The purpose of concentration is not a strained focussing of thought, but rather the elimination of the many and distracting thoughts and then finally even the division of thinker, object and thought. A successful concentration will unify the thought and focus it on a worthy object; in right meditation this unified thought will mature and ripen and finally dissolve into pure consciousness, which transcends all objects, outer or inner.

The aim of spiritual meditation, again, is not just focussing of the mind on anything and everything but on only that which helps in the unfoldment of holy virtues and the divine attributes like infinite purity, truth, knowledge, bliss and freedom. As such a holy personality, living, radiant and blissful would be a most desirable subject for meditation. One may start with an external representation, such as a picture or image but before long the 'chosen ideal' should go inside and must become one's inmost self, the soul of one's soul. In fact the holy, or divine personality should eventually take shape out of that radiant, blissful, living consciousness which is the essential core of the meditator himself.

*   *   *   *

Another problem raised by meditators is that relating to the formless aspect and to making the mind 'blank'. Holy life, spiritual life, God, truth are all whole and positive entities and one should beware of slipping into wrong implementations when apparently negative terms are used, or practices indicated.

The ultimate aim is to rise above all limitations, from the partial to the whole, and as such both our ideal as well as our practices should be oriented accordingly. 'Formless' is to be rather taken as that which is not limited by any particular form. Making the mind 'blank' should not mean becoming thoughtless or going to sleep; it is freeing the mind from all partial truths and distracting thoughts, so that pure consciousness alone, self-effulgent and blissful, manifests itself spontaneously, making one experience real inner calm, power and peace. Renunciation is giving up of the lower in favour of the higher, the smaller for the larger, the finite for the Infinite. Going inwards means, detaching oneself from all the external coverings, hiding and distorting the blessed reality of the Self.

Samādhi is being established in the consciousness of one's glorious infinite and inmost self or 'divinity'. Meditation is the continual current of pure thought in this direction to the exclusion of others. Concentration is the attempt to repeatedly bring back the thoughts from wandering away from this one Divine Self and externalising, and to holding it on the holy object. Steady posture and rhythmic breathing

are meant to make the body and nerves calm
and fit for the ensuing mental exercise.

     *   *   *

And much depends upon what kind of
person is he who has taken his seat to start
meditation. It will soon be discovered in
many cases that while one may sit physically
unmoving, the mind may be in a whirl, pro-
testing and straining, 'meditation' becoming a
most tiring and exasperating experience, instead
of a relaxing and refreshing one. Why?

Because during the rest of the day, the mind
and senses have been allowed to pursue an
almost diametrically opposite path, going after
the transitory, petty objects, externalising,
stressing likes and dislikes, and continually
opening oneself to passions, sensual desires,
resentments and greed. The body and senses
have been pampered, nerves exhausted by self-
centred exertion or so-called pleasures. For
the practice of meditation to become fruitful
and joyous, it is very essential that as far as
possible one should also extend its mood over
the rest of the day. Moderate and self-
controlled in food, sleep, activities and recreation, striving to be simple and honest, kind and
chaste, non-acquisitive and generous, cultiva-

ting an attitude of contentment and patience and reverent self-surrender to the Lord, and keeping the mind ever alert and discriminating, one will find it a joy to go in for meditation; one will find it a real blessing, really fruitful.

And finally, another distraction which plagues many aspirants—viz. measuring how far they have 'progressed'. Let it be remembered that real meditation is not a journey to anywhere else, it is not even a pilgrimage to some distant holy land. Even when it is described as an 'inner' pilgrimage it is but figurative and indicatory. We only reach and become our own divine Self. We only become aware of what we really are all along. It is a question of giving up the wrong, distracting thoughts, feelings, actions. The only progress is to intensify the thought of the 'Sat', the real, good and auspicious which is our very stuff and core. It is healthy not to be diverted by even these distractions which come in the form of a frequent desire to measure and judge one's progress. Nowhere perhaps is Bhagavan Sri Krishna's teaching on Karma Yoga so relevant as in this context: "Your concern is with the work on hand—never with the results." Leave the care and anxieties about the results to the

Lord, who is none other than the Soul of your
soul—and with a quiet and confident, yet humble
and reverent, faith apply yourself to the *sādhana*.
And be not surprised if unconsciously and
unheralded, you slide into perfection!

———o———

MEDITATION AND SPIRITUAL ENLIGHTENMENT

DR. ANIMA SEN GUPTA

The sages of the Upanishads have a firm faith in the essentially spiritual nature of man. Hence, in their opinion, the true purpose of human life is to realise this essential nature. The method for this purpose, as suggested by them, consists of Sravana, Manana and Nididhyāsana.

Sravana is not merely hearing the truth from the preceptor. It also implies ascertainment of the fact that the Sruti establishes the one Brahman without the second. Manana or reflection refers to (i) rational thinking on self or Brahman already heard from the preceptor and (ii) removal of all doubt by rational argumentations. Nididhyāsana is constant musing on self or Brahman. The quest for the self is the real quest of the human life and realisation of one's own nature as self or pure consciousness is the final goal.

Purpose of Life

So long as man is not aware of who he
is or what his true nature is, he is not in a
position to realise fully the meaning and
purpose of his life as man. He is unable to
apprehend his final fulfilment and is also
ignorant of his real good. Owing to utter
ignorance about the true nature of his being,
he is also unfit for the realisation of his real
relation with the world as a result of which his
reactions to the world are generally confused
and often become perverted. In other words,
a man is not able to determine correctly his
purpose and position in the world without
having a clear knowledge of his own self. If
he possesses wrong knowledge about himself,
then his perspective of the world is bound to
be vitiated. His value-sense, too, gets confused
and he moves on the ocean of life precariously
in the absence of appropriate guiding principles.

The Upanishads have declared repeatedly
that man is nothing but the self infinite (*Tat
tvam asi*). If this meaningful saying of the
Upanishads can be grasped fully by a man,
then he is sure to get inspired and is also sure
to undertake an enquiry into the nature of

his own true being. Sankara, too, has advised us to enquire into the meaning of *tvam* at the outset of our search for Truth. The search for the knowledge of self, however, involves self-analysis which is to be carried out rationally and in a regulated manner. If an aspirant can follow the path laid down by the Upanishads, with single-minded devotion, then only can he realise that beyond the conscious and the sub-conscious levels, there is another horizon of pure consciousness which constitutes the horizon of his real life. Nididhyāsana or repeated meditation on this illuminating light, opens the doors of his perception and he becomes fully conscious of his own true being. When repeated musing becomes so deep that thought process on the nature of the self appears as an unbroken flow, then this is called Meditation or Dhyāna. The Yoga-sūtra 3.2 has thus defined Meditation:

"*Tatra pratyaikatānatā dhyānam*" Meditation yields psychical power which can be utilised to obtain knowledge of any object of quest. It enables a man to have a correct and expert knowledge about the object of meditation. In meditation, only a single idea is present and the knowledge is continuous.

Discipline Of Meditation

To have correct knowledge of the self,
meditation, therefore, is essential. It is the
discipline of meditation that leads to the
intuitive realisation of the spiritual truth in
man. The psychical power, yielded by the
process of meditation, illumines the mind
from within and this inner illumination, then
reveals to the meditator, the secrets of his
real being and his relation to the world. It
is only when this secret is revealed that an aspirant can understand fully that he is not a
merely physical being, having only an unconscious heritage like other material things
of the world. He is also not merely psycho-
physical in nature as he appears to be, from a
superficial point of view. Both physical and
psychical aspects are "not-self aspects", which
have no essential and inseparable relation with
this true self. Self or spiritual light is his true
essence which lies beyond these physical and
psychical aspects of his personality. The true
'I' is the pure consciousness, unconditioned
by space, time and causation. It is different
from the empirical ego which is the real actor
in the drama of the world. It is only the
knowledge of the self which can make a man

free from all false notions that he has
up through ages of conditioning. Such
knowledge, however, cannot be gained with
meditation. Beyond the physical and the
psychical, a man must go to discover his immortal spiritual being.

Meditation needs as its pre-requisites (i)
the purification of the mind and the intellect,
and (ii) full control over the body and sense-
organs. The body, mind and the intellect
should become *Sāttvika* and it is the *Sāttvika*
Buddhi which is the only mirror that can reveal
the self in its true form. Hence, in his attempt
to discover his own true being, a man has got to
acquire moral qualities on the awakening of
which the impurities of the intellect, emotion
and will are completely wiped out. Moral
good is closely and essentially linked with the
good of the spirit. One who meditates on the
true nature of the self and has his intellect,
emotion and will purified and harmoniously
balanced, naturally becomes a man of eleva-
ted personality. He is regarded as a spiritually enlightened soul. With his enlightenment, he can visualise himself and the world
around him correctly and clearly and the
horizon of his spiritual vision becomes wide

and universal. The world, then, unfolds itself
in its true colour to the wise man and does not
therefore cause uneasiness to his mind. Thus
one who seeks to know the truth, must, first
of all, make his mind pure and well balanced.
Spiritual enlightenment, attained through meditation, pre-supposes moral awakening and
moral progress of man. The mind of the
meditator becomes calm and steady through
constant practice of meditation. His mind does
not get disturbed even in the midst of the vortex
created continuously by the waves of the
worldly life. The external world, with all its
vibrating currents, is always viewed by him
as external and is never identified with the
inner world. Such a person is truly perfect
and he never entertains any sort of illusion
regarding the relation of the world with man.
In fact, to enjoy the world in a detached but
lively way is the real art of living. It enables
the perfected personality to put necessary
limitations and restraints on the different
forms of enjoyment of the world. This he
can do, because he understands life from a deep
awareness of his spiritual nature which has been
revealed to him through meditation on his own
true form.

We should remember that meditation and spiritual enlightenment are essential not only for those gifted persons who embrace the life of total renunciation or Sannyasa, but also for all ordinary people, involved in active wordly life. One cannot achieve real greatness in the mundane life without being able to control his mind and sense organs and without having a correct awareness of himself and the world. It is only when a man can attain the state of control and steadiness of the mind that he can hope to reach the apex of glory of his empirical life and can discover that he has acquired the power of making even the insignificant events of the world happy and cheerful. He has freed himself from the clutches of his lower ego and has attained the power of looking at the world in an objective way. In fact, to be free from the clutches of a low, self-centred perspective of life is real freedom and this real freedom cannot be enjoyed if one is not spiritually enlightened. It is only in the state of his spiritual awareness that a man rises above the level of his limited individual self and prepares himself for the noble task of sacrificing his good and acting with energy and devotion for the good of the world. When a man can grasp clearly the distinction between the changing lower self and the unchangeable higher one, he attains the power of sacrificing his smaller ends for higher goals of life, whether empirical or transempirical.

To make sincere efforts to have a vision of the unchangeable and unaffected self of man is what is regarded as spiritual *Sādhanā* according to Indian tradition, and this *Sādhanā* in due course, finds its completion in spiritual enlightenment. Meditation is an essential limb of the spiritual discipline, because through meditation alone, man can discover his indwelling consciousness as his real being. When this spiritual gain is attained, a man is in a position to perform all his actions from a sacred sense of duty which is not linked with any egoistic motive of gain, arrogance, hatred and pride. A mind which is free from all impurities of thought, emotion and will is a healthy mind and its attitude towards the world is also a healthy one in the sense that he lives his life in this world in a planned and organized manner which is in tune with his own spiritual being. He understands in proper perspective his duties and responsibilities to others as well as to himself. He is prepared to discharge them sincerely so as to be able to promote

effectively the solidarity and enduring welfare
of society. The Mahābhārata has asserted
that good character and good behaviour are
the result of true knowledge and to attain true
knowledge, one has to practise meditation along
with all its necessary parts. Disciplined mind
and virtuous conduct are the results of true
knowledge of the self and the world. Spiritual
awakening does not inspire a man to shun the
world completely. On the other hand, the
spiritual training makes a man conscious of
his true being as a result of which he can link
his empirical life with his life of the spirit in a
harmonious and fruitful way. The self-knowledge gives him strength and courage to face
the world. His soul being purified by true
knowledge, he returns to active life with a
longing to do good to the whole of mankind.
Swami Vivekananda has said: "The spiritual
ideal is for life and this must be lived in all
spheres, private, social and international."

Yogic Postures

In the present age, a great emphasis is being
laid on the practice of Yogic postures as a form
of highly effective physical exercise for keeping
the body healthy and also for driving out
germs of diseases from it. This no doubt is a

very laudable step, because nobody can do any good work without being the possessor of a healthy body. Again, if a man fails to preserve his physical health in a proper manner, his mental health too suffers degeneration. Practice of Yogic postures is very efficacious in curing physical illnesses of different kinds.

If, however, we get interested only in the practice of yogic postures with the sole aim of keeping our body healthy and do not make efforts to cure our mind from perverse thoughts and emotions, then our confused mind is sure to exert adverse influences on our physica' frame. It is only when a man is ignorant of his true, immortal being that he becomes an easy prey to egoism, greed, hatred, fear, etc., which make his mind unhealthy and unhelpful. With such a diseased mind, nobody can hope to do any good work in his social life. A man should not only be physically healthy but he should also be spiritually awakened. The material basis of life is intimately connected with its spiritual flowering and so it is necessary for a man to have a healthy mind in a healthy body.

The ardent followers of Yogic postures

have, no doubt, realised to a certain extent the need for the steadiness of mind which they aim at attaining through concentration (*dhāraṇā*), but they have failed to realise that this concentration should be directed to the realisation of the true nature of man and not to the things of the material world. Concentration on the things of the material world only, may result in an increase in the power of vision, but it will not enable the aspirant to grow in knowledge and pure emotions. The goal of Yoga is self-realisation which enlightens and elevates the mind and character of the Yogin. This is spiritual achievement that enables him to discover the higher truth which is embedded in him. He can also grasp fully the meaning and purpose of life and can develop a dispassionate love and liking for things and beings of the world. When spiritual enlightenment penetrates each and every corner of a man's multi-coloured life, he becomes a truly balanced person of profound serenity, who is in a position to overcome all divisions and rifts which trouble mundane life. Such an enlightened person alone can develop a liberal outlook and a spirit of toleration so as to be able to accommodate others' views and others' needs. He gives

up the habit of hankering after wealth and
property and whatever he does, he does for
the good of mankind. It is only when a man
can realise his essentially immortal nature
which is wholly unaffected by colourful waves
of the world that he can cultivate a detached
but highly tender attitude towards life and the
world. We should not forget that there is no
gap between the empirical and the transempirical. The transempirical is to be sought by
remaining in a social order and promoting
social good. The empirical life, if led thought-
fully in the light of spiritual wisdom, will find its
spontaneous completion in the transempirical
state of liberation.

Hence, it is desirable that in adopting Yogic
postures as a technique for healthy living, both
concentration and meditation on self should be
adopted as essential parts along with all other
moral practices. The method of Rāja Yoga
is moral through and through, because without
the destruction of impurities of thought, will
and emotion, the mind can never be turned
towards self-knowledge. The five forms of
restraints which constitute the first limb of
Yoga are moral restraints. Again *tapas* (which
is essential) implies moral discipline and

control over thoughts, feelings and actions. Awakening of true knowledge through purification of mind is imperative, if the health of the mind is to be preserved.

What, after all, is our aim in practising Yogic postures as a form of exercise? We definitely want to be good and healthy members of the human society with noble tendencies and inspiring thoughts and emotions. Yoga should therefore, be followed as a practical method for the development of both the body and the mind in such a manner that higher fields of experience may be opened to the person who practises it. This will necessitate incorporation of concentration and meditation on higher truth of life so as to gain spiritual enlightenment. The Yogic training should give not only a physical poise but also an insight into the real nature of the self and the world, so that the practitioner may be able to cultivate correct attitudes towards all things and beings of the universe. In order to enjoy beauty and bliss through all relations which exist between man and man, one should not only be physically healthy but should also have a calm and pure mind, shining with the glow of knowledge and truth.

MEDITATION:
A SCIENTIFIC APPRAISAL

DR. SAMPOORAN SINGH

The superficial conscious mind is occupied with its daily activities, with earning a livelihood, deceiving others, exploiting others, running away from problems—all the petty daily activities of our existence. To observe and understand our hidden motives, responses, thoughts and feelings, there must be tranquillity in the conscious mind, so that the deep layers of the sub-conscious mind are projected at the conscious level. The mind cannot bring about tranquillity, stillness, peace by mere regimentation, by compulsion, by discipline; it can bring it about only by understanding its own activities, by observing them, by being aware of them. The right understanding of the deepest inner layers of the subconscious mind—the racial instincts, the animal instincts, the concealed pursuits will bring tranquillity and stillness; when the whole mind is unconditioned, unburdened, unfettered by all past memories, then it is in a state to receive the eternal. It is only through dispassionate observation and feelingful-understanding that this tangle can be unravelled and order can prevail. This is real meditation—understanding the nature of thought, not verbally but with our whole being. It is being aware of what is going on without any distortion, without any choice, without any resentment, bitterness, explanation or justification—the mind must just be aware. Meditation is to observe every movement of thought, attentive to its every detail.

Meditation is to see the fact in totality. The very seeing of it is the action; and for that one needs a clear, sharp, sensitive mind, which comes from intelligent awareness. The mind must act without any resistance, without any form of friction. Resistance is conflict, division. Resistance creates other forms of distortion, violence begets more violence. To see or observe a fact is to understand it·in its totality; it is not a matter of overcoming or suppressing its resistance; true observing is a resistanceless or frictionless flow. Then the mind is meditative.

Since Nature is really one and our mind is part of it, it would be interesting to study the parallelism between the psychological field of the mind and the field of energy as comprehended by modern physics.

Superconductivity: One of the most powerful methods discovered for working out the fine details of solid structure is through the use of very low temperatures. Under these conditions the thermal fluctuations of the lattice become small and effects which would not otherwise be noticed become obvious. Superconduction, which is the vanishing of resistivity as the temperature approaches $O°K$, is shown by a number of elements, such as zinc, gallium, titanium, cadmium, mercury, lead, tin and niobium, and many alloys and compounds. The flow of electric current without resistance at sufficiently low temperatures in certain solids is called superconductivity. In superconductivity, the specimen undergoes a phase transition from a state of normal electrical resistivity to a superconducting state. The temperature at which the resistance disappears, in zero magnetic field, is called the transition temperature. The transition occurs over a very narrow temperature range. Its onset takes place at the highest temperature 11.2° Absolute in the metal technetium and at 7.2° Absolute in lead. In a superconductor an electric charge can pass without any measurable voltage between its ends. The extent to which the flow of electric current in a superconductor is frictionless has been demonstrated by an experiment in which a persistent electric current has been observed to flow without measurable decrease in amplitude around a superconducting lead ring for over 2 years. If a bar magnet is lowered near a lead dish which is at the temperature of liquid helium ($-452°$ F), it hovers in the air, the chain slack. The magnet has induced a current in the lead; as it meets no resistance, the lead becomes a powerful electromagnet, repelling and holding the magnet above. Very strong magnetic fields destroy superconductivity, and the strength of a field that does this is a function of the temperature. This leads to the belief that the phenomenon is related in some fashion to the magnetic properties of the material. As a matter of fact, conductors in the superconducting state exhibit perfect diamagnetic properties.

Superfluidity: The behaviour of liquefied helium when it is cooled below $2.1°$ Absolute is most surprising, and this frictionless flow of matter is called "superfluidity". Liquid helium can flow without any apparent friction through slits so small that ordinary liquids and gases can hardly pass through. The liquid gas flows with ease through the finest capillaries and will siphon itself out of a container by flowing uphill in a film which quickly climbs over the container walls.

Parallels Between Mind and Modern Physics: The strange world of absolute zero showing frictionless flow of matter (Superfluidity) and flow of electric current without resistance (superconductivity) appears to have fascinating correspondences with the resistanceless and frictionless state of the mind. The parallels are: First, just as the properties of the material, *e.g.,* superfluidity and superconductivity, change within one hundredth of a degree centigrade, similarly the characteristics of the mind change when mind moves from a state having resistance to a resistanceless state. Second, the sudden transformation of properties in matters appears to be related in some fashion to the magnetic properties of the material and change of the ions in the metallic lattice, but these transformations are far from clear. Similarly the sudden transformation of the characteristics of the state of mind with resistance to a state of mind without resistance appears to be due to some psychomagnetic changes (cortical neuronal changes) and change of circuitory due to some flip-flop switches, but we know nothing about it. It is an example of weak causality in the microcosmic region. Third, the strange world of absolute zero exists at the material plane. It appears that the properties of matter at low temperatures are controlled by the new set of physical laws which are necessary to describe atomic behaviour. The new set of physical laws will take into consideration the behaviour of elements and their compounds when the friction or the resistance is zero. The mind without resistance or without friction bestows on us the pure perception and gives us vision of the Absolute, the Truth. Thus the Truth selfmanifests at the subtlest plane. It is not amenable to an experimental verification even with the help of the latest artifacts, due to its subtlest plan.

The movement of the mind from a state with resistance to a state without resistance is called the quantum jump of the mind from logical and scientific reason to unfettered philosophical reason; or from relative state (conscious state) to an absolute state (super-

conscious state); or it is a leap from the lower
plane of relational knowledge (intellectual
knowledge) to a higher plane of ultrarelational
knowledge (intuitional knowledge). As there
is no matter which is self-effulgent,so we assume
that the neurons of the mind receive illumination from the self-effulgent Self, the Atman, the
Universal Consciousness. The state of mind
with resistance is capable of receiving partial
illumination, a state of mind without resistance
is capable of receiving full illumination from the
Self and as such is fully illumined with the
pristine glory of the Self, and as such is fully
bathed with truth. The state of mind without resistance is capable of pure perception
and as such the mind perceives the present
moment of the chronological space-time continuum, and there is a continuous flow of
the present moment only, this is the vision of
the Absolute where there is neither time,
space, nor causation. This is the realisation
of the eternal values in the chronological space-
time continuum, which means, the attainment
of the state of detachment, selfless service and
eternal love for the entire humanity.

Meditation is a liberation from the resistance of the mind, which is the past condi-

tioning. It is a movement of the state of mind with resistance to a state without resistance, or in other words to transcend the past and live in the present only.

The conditioning is due to the psychological knowledge, memories, total thought process, which implies resistance. Intelligence implies freedom, which means that intelligence will use knowledge when necessary and yet be free from knowledge. Meditation is the ending of resistance, which means ending of psychological knowledge, memoires, the past, the observer. The state of mind without resistance functions in a different dimension altogether which is intelligence. Intelligence implies freedom; freedom implies the cessation of all conflicts; intelligence comes into being and conflict comes to an end when the "observer" is the observed, for then there is no division, no resistance, no friction; this is the self-manifestation of love. Love can only come into being when there is real freedom from the past as knowledge. Meditation is a movement from resistance to resistancelessness, from friction to frictionlessness, from psychological knowledge to intelligence, from bondage to freedom.

ACKNOWLEDGEMENT

I have drawn freely from the thoughts of Swami Vivekananda, Edwin Schrodinger, Albert Einstein, Dr. Fritjof Capra, and Krishna-murthi in composing this article.

—O—

MEDITATION ACCORDING TO MAZDAYASNA (Zoroastrianism)

B.S. SURTI

Introduction

Mazdayasna attaches very great importance to Meditation.

A human being is a conglomerate of three functions, *viz.,* **Thoughts, Words,** and **Deeds.** Mazdayasna gives the first place to **Thoughts** (Meditation) because it comes first in order of sequence, *e.g.,* a man first thinks, then he reveals his **Thoughts** in words, spoken or written or both, and finally he translates his avowal into action. This sequence is always maintained in the immutable Divine scheme of things although in some cases the thinking may be so shallow or lacking so much in depth that a person's words or deeds may appear to have sprung spontaneously without any thinking at all. Whenever we say that a certain person is incapable of thinking what we mean is that that person is not capable of deep or serious thinking (Meditation). It is obvious

12

that words and deeds arising out of deep and
serious thinking (Meditation) will be a higher
quality, and more responsible in nature, than
those springing from shallow and frivolous
thinking, *i.e.,* absence of Meditation. Therefore
speaking or writing or performing deeds without
Meditation is considered to be an irresponsible
or irreligious act according to Mazdayasna.

Saadi (1184-1292 A.D.), in his Persian
classic "Gulistaan" which is still regarded as
a model of choicest Persian prose writing,
relates the following story:—

A deputation of learned men from India
had gone to the court of Emperor Naosheerwaan the Just (531-579 A.D.) of Iran, called
Chosroes I by Greeks, whose sense of Justice
and Impartiality has been praised by the
Holy Prophet Mohammad. They held dis-
cussions there with Naosheerwaan's Prime
Minister, Buzurgmeher, considered to be the
wisest man of all ages. When asked to express
their opinion about Buzurgmeher's reputed
wisdom, the Indian savants declared that he
was flawless except for the fact that he took
a long time to answer any question, thereby
taxing the listeners' patience. When Buzurg-

meher was informed of this he explained:
**"To think what I should say is better than to
repent why I said it"**. Saadi sermonizes on the
basis of the story:

**"Sakhundaan-e parwardah
peer-e-kuhan"**

(An experienced and cultured con-
versationalist)

**"Ba-yendeeshad, angaah
ba-gooyad sukhan"**

(Thinks, and then speaks)

"Mazan bi-taammul ba guftaar dam"

(Do not open your mouth to speak,
without reflection)

**"Neko gooy, gar deer gooyi cheh
gham?"**

(Answer rightly and to the point;
what harm is there if you do so
somewhat late?)

**"Be-yendeesh o angah bar aavar
nafas"**

(Think well, and then open your
mouth to speak)

"**Vazaan peesh bas kun keh
      gooyand bas**"
(And stop speaking before the audi-
        ence asks you to stop).

Meditation should be Positive or Constructive

According to Mazdayasna, Meditation for
the sake of Meditation is of no value. Meditation should always be a means of expression
in words (spoken and/ or written) and of performance of deeds, and not an end in itself.

It is clear that the quality of words and
deeds will depend upon the quality of Meditation. Negative and Destructive thinking, called
Dush-mata in Avesta, will lead to words that
will injure the feelings, called **Duzh-ukta** in
Avesta, and to deeds that will pollute the body,
debase the mind, and dampen the spirit of the
thinker as well as that of the persons around
him. Such a deed is called **Duzh-varshta** in
Avesta.

That is why Mazdayasna places the utmost
emphasis on Positive Constructive thinking,
called **Hu-mata** in Avesta. **Hu-mata** by itself,
is useless unless it is followed by **Hu-ukta** *i.e.,*

Positive or Constructive words, and **Hu-varshta,** *i.e.,* Positive or Constructive deeds.

Importance of Righteous Meditation

Since Thought Force is capable of limitless possibilities and potentialities, both for Good and for Evil, Mazdayasna severely warns against evil thinking and exhorts Righteous thinking with single-minded devotion and concentration. The Holy Prophet Zara-thushtra, while meditating on the top of Mount Ushidarena, exerted his utmost at every step to ward off evil thoughts and licentious reveries that were threatening to overpower him. It was only after fifteen years of superhuman struggle with evil thoughts that he felt that he had conquered evil passions and harmful emotions sufficiently to come down from the mountain, and proclaim to the world:—

"**Vispa Hu-mata, Vispa Hu-ukta Vispa Hu-Varshta baodho varshta**".

(All Righteous Thoughts and their sequelae, *viz,* all Righteous Words, and all Righteous Deeds, spring from Wisdom).

"**Vispa Dush-mata, Vispa Duzh-ukta, Vispa Duzh-varshta,** *noit*

baodho varshta".

(All evil thoughts—and their sequelae
such as—all evil words, all evil deeds
do not spring from Wisdom).

(Prayer in Khordeh Avesta)

Henceforth, therefore, in the course of
this article, the word "Meditation" should be
understood as meaning Righteous Meditation,
Hu-mata and not evil meditation, Dushmata.

The seat or source of Meditation is the Mind,
called **Mano** or *Manas* in Avesta. Since it is
Righteous Meditation that we are extolling,
the Mind which is the seat or source of such
meditation is called **Vohu Mano** (Righteous
Mind).

In one of the three most ancient Mazdayasnian prayers, dating back to thousands of
years before Zarathushtra, known as **Ahuna
Vairya** it is revealed:

"**Vanghe-ush dazdaa Manangh-ho, shyo-
thana-naam anghe-ush Mazdaa-ee**".

(Righteous Meditation enables one to
do Righteous Deeds for the Good
of the creation and the Glory of God)
(Yas. 27 : 13)

Zarathushtra, himself, exhorts his followers in the following words:—

> 'Sarotaa- ge-ooshaa-eesh vahishtaa"
>
> (Hear properly with your ears)

> "Ava-entaa soochaa mananghaa"
>
> (Meditate with Pure Mind)

> "Avare-naao viochith-hyaa narem narem khakhyaa-ee tanoo-ye"
>
> (Let every man, individually, choose what is best for himself).
>
> (Yas. 30: 2)

Zarathushtra reveals, thus, the importance of Righteous Meditation in upholding the dignity of the individual, and in not following blindly what others say without thinking for oneself. Faith without Reason is prohibited according to Zarathushtra's interpretation of Mazdayasna.

Zarathushtra's Yearning for Righteous Meditation.

Zarathushtra prays to God:—

> "Daao Ashaa Vanghe-ush maayaa-o Manangh-ho"
>
> (Give us Purity through Righteous Mind [Meditation].) (Yas. 43 : 2)

Again, he prays:—

"Daaeedi Ashaa taam Asheem Vanghe-ush aayaptaa Manangh-ho"

(Give us Purity which is the reward for Righteous Mind, *i.e.,* Meditation).

(Yas. 28 : 7)

As an earnest pupil imploring his teacher, Zarathushtra pleads with Ahura Mazda (Avestan name for God):—

"Sees haa naao Ashaa patho Vanghe-ush khwaitengh Manangh-ho"

(Yas 34 : 12)

(Teach us the path of Purity through Righteous Mind, i.e. Meditation)   (Yas. 34 : 12)

So impatient is he to attain Purity that he finds it difficult to exercise self-control and exclaims in desparation:—

"Ashaa kwat thwaa daresaani Manascha Vohu va-e-demno"?

(Purity! when shall I see thee through the eyes of Righteous Mind. *i.e.* Meditation?)

(Yas. 28:5

So much importance is given to Purity that it is regarded as the only Path to God realization:—

"Aevo Pantaao, yo Ashahe;
Vispe anyeshaam apantaam"

(There is only one path, that of Purity; all others are no paths.)

(Yas. 72 : 11)

Ahura Mazda and Amesha Spentas.

Observant readers might have noticed in the Gatha passage quoted above, just before last, and must have wondered why, Zarathushtra, instead of asking Ahura Mazda as is his wont, addresses Purity (**Ashaa**) directly in this case! To understand the rationale and logic of Zarathushtra's action one must have a clear-cut idea of the term **Amesha pentas.** Amesha means immortal. Spenta means Holy. **Amesha Spentas,** therefore, can be translated as Immortal Holies. Who or what are these Immortal Holies? and how many are they?

Answering the second question first, they are seven in number, hence they are called Haft Amesha Spentas, haft means seven. The nature of the **Amesha Spentas** will become manifest as we describe the seven one by one:—

The first and foremost of the seven is named
Ahura Mazda. **Ahu** means Life or Spirit, from
the root "**Ah**" meaning "to be". "**Ra**" means
"giver". The Sanskrit equivalent of **Mazda**
is "**Mahada**", ("**Maha**" meaning "great", and
"**da**" meaning "give". **Ahura Mazda,** therefore
means "Life giver, the Great giver", *i.e.,* "the
Great Creator". So, **Creation is the first and
foremost and most important attribute of Gods.**

2. The second attribute is called **Vohu
Mano. Vohu** means Righteous, and **Mano**
means Mind which is the source of Meditation.
Vohu Mano,therefore, means Righteous Medita-
tion. It is thus obvious that Mazdayasna
attaches so much importance to Righteous
Meditation as to consider it to be a Divine
Quality.

3. We have already quoted from the Ga-
thas that Righteous Mind (Meditations) leads
to Purity (**Ashaa**). The third Divine attribute,
therefore, is **Asha Vahista**, **Ashaa** meaning
Purity, and **Vahishta** meaning highest or 'in
excelsis'. Hence **Asha Vahishta** means Purity
in excelsis.

4. Armed with Righteous Mind (Meditation) and the Highest Purity, one is fit to exer-

cise Power as desired for the Good of the world and the Glory of God. Hence, the fourth Divine attribute is **Khshatra Vairya. Khshathra** means Power, **Vairya** means "desired". **Khshathra Vairya** means "Power as desired".

5. Righteous Mind (Meditation), a Pure Heart, and exercise of the desired Power cannot but foster Devotion which is another name for Love, fervour, rapture, enthusiasm, which is so essential for the Good of the World and the Glory of God. Hence the fifth Divine attribute is **Spenta Aarmaiti**. **Spenta** means Holy, and **Aarmaiti** means Devotion. **Spenta Aarmaiti,** therefore, means Holy Devotion or any of its equivalents mentioned above.

6. One who is equipped with Righteous Mind (Meditation), Pure Heart, Power or Potency, and Holy Devotion, can aspire to the sixth Divine characteristic, **Haurvataat** which means Perfection.

7. All the above six qualities make one eligible to aspire for the seventh Divine characteristic, **Amertaat** which means Immortality.

It must be noted that all the seven qualities mentioned above *viz.* : Creator, Righteous Meditator, Pure, Powerful, Devoted-Perfect, and Immortal, are to be found in toto in God Himself. The entire creation, including Human Beings, can only aspire to possess them but can never acquire them to the extent of one hundred per cent. The extent to which a human being tries his level best to approach this composite concept of Divinity marks him out as being Godly to that extent.

Meditation on Fire

As mentioned in my article "Essence of Mazdayasna (Zoroastrainism) in *Vedanta Kesari* of July, 1977, it is not possible for anyone except the most spiritually advanced souls to meditate on an abstract entity such as God. A concerete symbol is a '*sine qua non*' for fruitful meditation. Zarathushtra's exhortation to his listeners: **"Contemplate the Beams of Fire with a Most Pious Mind"** and the reasons why Fire is the most appropriate symbol of Divinity, and what all should one meditate about Fire, have been given in great detail in the article mentioned above.

In the Avestan Prayer, **"Aatash Niyayash"** (Salutation to Fire) it is mentioned:—

"Vispa-e-eebio sasteem baraiti Aatarsh
    Mazdaa-o Ahura-he"

(Ahura Mazda's Fire carries a lesson for
    all).

Meditation on Immortality of Soul

If one believes in **Ahura Mazda** as the Universal Soul (**Paramaatman**) who is the sum total of all the souls (**Jeevaatmas**) in the entire creation, it automatically implies unqualified belief in the immortality of individual souls (**Jeevaatmas**). This teaching of Mazdayasna that there is a world of Matter, **Anghe-ush Astavaiti,** as well as a world of spirits, **Anghe-ush Mainyu,** has been corroborated by all the great religions and philosophies that followed Mazdayasna.

Meditation on Death

From the beginning of creation nothing has held people in greater awe or mystery than the phenomenon of Death. Mazdayasna was the first philosophical system to point out that so called Death is nothing but the discarding of its outer vesture, the body, by a soul in the same manner as one discards one's clothes. The only difference is that if the clothes are removed one can still see the body of the individual because clothes and body are, both, material, and can be easily seen with the physical eyes; whereas if an individual removes his own body one cannot see the soul since it is not material but etherial.

Although all religions are agreed about the immortality of the Soul or Spirit, different religions have different opinions about the immediate and ultimate goal of the Soul. According to some, the soul, liberated from a body, puts on a body of the same species, *i.e.,* after discarding one human body it puts on another human body. This goes by the name of **Re-incarnation.** After going through a number of such re-births, the highly evolved soul, **Jeevaatma,** finally merges into the Universal Spirit (**Paramaatman**).

According to some others, the soul, which discards a human body, may put on the body of another species, *e.g.,* an animal. This is called **Metempsychosis.**

No religion has clearly mentioned how long after discarding one body the soul puts on another.

According to Judaism, Christianity, and

Islam, each and everyone of the souls will arise from the grave in flesh and blood on the day of Resurrection, and be answerable for their deeds to God who will sentence them accordingly, to a permanent abode in Heaven or Hell.

Mazdayasna tells us that after shedding its mortal coil the soul passes away into the world of spirits to lead there either a happy or a sorrowful life depending upon its performance in the world of Matter. It remains for ever in the world of Spirits; but always ends its blessings upon us, invokes God's blessings upon us, and helps us to the best of its ability whenever we remember it in our sincere prayers to Ahura Mazda and invoke His blessings upon it. It yearns and feels happy to be remembered by those with whom it was in close contact in the world of Matter.

So, according to Mazdayasna, so called Death is only a *"passing away"* of the soul from the world of Matter into the world of Spirits. The great Mazdayasni poet, Firdausi (935-1025 A.D.) advises human beings:—

"Ze roos-e guzar kardan andeeshah kun"

(Think of the day when you shall pass away)

"Parasteedan-e Daadgar peeshah kun"
(Make worship of God your profession
and way)

"Ba neeki garaay-o mayaazaar kas"
(Indulge in Righteousness and harm no
one)

"Ra-he rastagaari hameenast o bas"
(That is how your salvation will be won).

Regarding the Mazdayasnian conception of
Immortality of Spirit and the desire of the
soul not to be forgotten by us, the Mazdayasni poet, Nizaami Ganjawi (1140-1203
A.D.) clarifies:—

"Fishaani tu bar man sarishki ze door"
(Shower a tear from afar on me)

"Fishaanam man az aasmaan bar tu noor"
(And Heaven its blessings will shower on
thee)

"Duaa-e tu bar har cheh daarad shitaab"
(Whatever thy sincere desires may be)

"Man aameen kunam taa shavad mustajaab"
(I'll say "Amen", they granted may be)

"Daroodam rasaani, rasaanam darood"
(Send thou thy prayers, and I shall send
mine)

"**Biyaa-ee, biyaayam ze gumbad farood**"
  (Come here and I'll come from this tomb
    of mine)

"**Maraa zindah pindaar choon kheeshtan**"
  (Consider me as alive as thou art)

"**Man aayam ba jaan gar tu aayee ba tan**"
  (I'll come with my soul if you come with
    your heart)

"**Madaan khaali as hamnasheeni maraa**"
  (Think not that bereft of friends I may
    be)

"**Keh beenam turaa gar na beeni maraa**"
  (If you cannot see me, I can see thee)

"**Lab az khufta-e chand khaamush makun**"
  (Let not thy lips cease to praise those
    who slept)

"**Farookhuftagaan raa faraamush makun**"
  (Forget, O never, all those who have slept).

A Mazdyasni poet of the Pahlavi regime,
whose poetic pen name is Spenta, after frankly
confessing that one does not know the purpose
of one's earthly existence, where we come from,
and whither we go after our earthly existence is
over, draws the analogy of a ray of the Sun
which, temporarily, gets obscured by a passing
cloud and gets cut off from the Sun. Once the

cloud passes away, the ray of light once again rejoins the Sun. The poet wishes to convey through this charming analogy the idea of an individual soul, **Jeevaatma,** merging into the Universal Spirit, **Paramaatman.** Here is how he sings:—

"**Nadaaneem azeen jaa kujaa mee raveem**"
    (We know not, from here, whither do
      we go)

"**Charaa aamadeem o charaa mee raveem.**"
    (Why did we come and why do we go.)

"**Kas asz sarr-e een raah aagaah neest**"
    (The secret of this has been revealed to
      none)

"**Pas-e pardah kas raa digar raah neest**"
    (Behind the curtain there is access to
      none)

"**Judaa shud yeki zarrah az aaftaab**"
    (A ray of light from the Sun strayed away)

"**Nehaan maand yekchand andar sahaab**"
    (And remained in the cloud quite hidden
      away)

"**Chu az teerah-goon ab re- hasti guzasht**"
    (When it from the cloud of existence
      emerged)

"**Ze khirsheed-e taabindah paivastah gasht**"
    (Into the radiant Sun it merged).

Conclusion.

We may conclude with a quotation from the famous Physiologist and Nobel Laureate Alexis Carrel. We have taken the liberty of substituting the word "Meditation" for "Prayer" in Carrel's original.

"Meditation is the most powerful form of energy that one can generate. The influence of Meditation on the human mind and body is as demonstrable as that of secreting glands. Its results can be measured in terms of increased physical buoyancy, greater intellectual vigour moral stamina and a deeper understanding of the realities underlying human relationships. True Meditation is a way of life; the truest life is literally a way of Meditation."

—O—

MEDITATION ACCORDING TO SUFISM

SWAMI PRABHANANDA

Tradition claims that Sufism was developed by the Prophet Mohammed through
his cousin and son-in-law Ali Ibn Abi Taleb,
the fourth Caliph, whose abdication led finally
to the schism between Sunni and Shia. The
Prophet is said to have invested Ali with a
cloak of Kherqa and initiated him into the
esoteric mysteries. The Koran, the book of
Allah's revelation to Mohammed, contains
passages of a mystical nature and the Sufis
seized upon them 'to buttress their own claim
to personal trafficking with God.' As an
indispensable prerequisite to mystical communion, the ascetic outlook and practices charac-
terised the life of Mohammed himself and
many of his followers. Towards the end of the
8th century A.D. austere Muslims, whose lives
were consumed by the fire of God's love, cut
themselves off from the mundane world, and
devoted themselves to the recollection of God,
took to wearing wool to proclaim their other-

worldliness and were therefore nicknamed Sufis. Lexicographers, however, offer different interpretations of the word 'Sufi'. Bishr Ivn Al-Harit says, "The Sufi is he whose heart is *safa* (pure) towards God." According to others 'Sufis' are those who can be placed in the first rank or '*saff*' before God through the excellence of their spiritual development. Again, some others opine that Sufi comes from '*suffah*' which means a person who is not a slave of desires.

The genesis of Sufism emphasises the esoteric doctrine of the Prophet, as may be found in stray references in the Quran and the Hadis. Some consider it as a reaction of the Aryan mind against a Semitic religion thrust upon it. Some think that Plotinus, who visited Iran with seven neo-Platonist philosophers, exerted this influence on Islam in the time of Naushirwan and the result was the emergence of this faith. Sufism is based on Islamic faith which has six pillars: (a) God exists; (b) God is one; (c) there are Angels; (d) there are Prophets; (e) there is a day of restoration and (f) there is Fate.

Different interpretations of lexicographers

notwithstanding, the Sufis regard their Creator as their '*Leah*' or deity and worship Him alone and believe that there is none other than He and no other true relation that exists between them and their Creator. Sufis call the ideas of God, the "essences of things" which when created are called external objects or created things of the world. God is "one", His ideas are "many". Ideas depend on God for their existence but God exists independently. The essence of God is obviously different from the essence of created beings but there exists a relationship between the two.

Ideas of God or "essences" are uncreated, perfect and immutable. Every essence has its own characteristic which is called *Shakilat*. Ibn-Al-Arabi says, "Glory be to God who created things being Himself their essences." External beings derive their attributes like life, knowledge, will power, hearing, sight and speech from God alone. A Sufi in his highest realisation discovers that all these attributes are borrowed and metaphysically applied to himself, whereas they really belong to God.

Though existence is one, the essences are many. A true Sufi knows that he is internally but an idea in the mind of God and he is, therefore, co-eternal with God. Externally he is a created being. In him God has manifested Himself in accordance with the aptitudes or the *shakilat* of the Sufi.

The Sufistic doctrine that God is the only Being extant has been expressed by Jalaluddin Rumi in his *Masnavi*.

> If He makes me a cup, a cup am I,
> If He makes of me a dagger, a dagger I.
> .... ,....
> If He makes me fire, I give forth heat......
> If He makes me a friend,
>   I serve my friends.
> I am as the pen in the fingers
>   of the writer,
> I am not in a position to obey or not
>   at will.

The Reality is one, and all apparent multiplicity is but a mode of unity. An existence is merely an objectification of His essesence. This realisation is possible only with the progressive annihilation of the individual self which, encrusted with material dross, stands separate from God. The problem of evil has been dealt with by the Sufis in their charac-

teristic fashion. The universe is essentially
good. What man calls evil is privation, not-
being. In relation to the One it is nothing;
it appears only in the phenomenal world. A
pool of standing water becomes dirty when some
dirt is thrown into it; it takes the colour of
whatever it comes in contact with. However,
if it is joined with a perennially flowing stream,
it becomes purified sooner or later. Similarly
if an individual is able to get in contact with the
Universal Self, the individual's pettiness and
dross have no effect whatsoever on the path
of his spiritual progress.

Al-Junaid defined Sufism (*tasauwuf*), "God
should cause thee to die from thyself and live
in Him." The supreme mystical experience
consists in the passing away of the temporal
ego into the Eternal Ego. This dying off is
fana and the life-in-him is *baqā*. By the
elevation of the self the mystic is perfected,
transmuted and eternalised through God and
in God alone. Following the mystic's return
to the state in which he was before *i.e.*,
union with God, God separates him from
Himself and grants him his individuality again.
Al-Junaid writes:

> So in a manner we
> United are, and One;
> Yet otherwise disunion
> Is our estate eternally.

His contemporary Al-Hallaj's utterance, "I am the Truth" (*ana'l haqq*) illustrates how the intoxicated Sufi got absorbed in serving the will of God—but he was condemned for blasphemy and was brutally executed. Thereafter the majority of Sufis laboured to work out an understanding between Sufism and .traditionalism and accepted theology. Like Rābia of Basra, Dhal'l-Nun al-Mesi, the great mystic, fixed a tradition when he wrote,

> I die and yet not die in me,
> The ardour of my love for Thee,
> Nor hath Thy love, my only goal,
> Assuaged the fever of my soul.

The doctrine of passing away in God (*fana*) was successfully synthesized with the doctrine of Divine Unity.

Ahmed Al-Ghazali tried to reconcile Sufism with Muslim orthodoxy. He emphasised that the Muslim life of devotion to the One God could not be lived perfectly save by following the

'Sufi' way. In his master-piece, "*Ihyā' utum al-din*" (Revival of religious science) he succeeded in assuring the mystical or introspective attitude a place within the framework of official Islam side by side with the legalism of the lawyers and the intellectualism of theologians. The Logos doctrine states that God's vice-regent controlling the internal material universe is the "Idea of Muhammad". If a man aspires to know God he may first achieve union with the "Idea of Muhammad", projected by God in pre-eternity to be His likeness and to lead mankind back to Him. This idea was fully developed by Ibn al-Farid of Cairo.

Muhyi al-Din Ib'n Arabi was the greatest mystical genius of the Arabs. Following Ib'n Arabi's conception of the Unity of Being (*wahdat al-wajūd*), Abd al-Karim al-Jil traces the descent of the pure Being through three stages of Oneness (*ahadiya*), He-ness (*hu-wiya*), and I-ness (*anīya*) and points out that this path can be retraced through corresponding stages of illumination (*tajallī*) till he becomes the Perfect Man, being shorn of attributes, and returns once more as Absolute to the Absolute.

Sufism centres on the questions, *i.e.,* (a) How

is man to realize God in himself? and (b) What is God in relation to the individual and the creation? Sufism offers *tariqat* in answer to the first and imparts *ma'rifat* or knowledge which describes God, in answer to the second. It is obvious that importance is attached more to the inner self and its activities than the outward religious practices and rituals.

Sufi psychology, so far as it bears on the ecstatic life, focusses attention to (a) *nafs*, the appetitive soul; (b) *ruh*, the spirit; (c) *qalb*, the heart and (d) *'aql*, the intelligence. The *nafs*, being the seat of passions, is to be fought by means of asceticism. The *qalb* and the *ruh*, though they cannot be clearly distinguished from one another, are the organs the mystic depends upon for his spiritual growth. *Qalb* is a non-material essence whereby the realities of all things are perceived as in a mirror. The more the heart is free from sin, egoism, traditional beliefs etc., the vision of reality becomes more perfect. God alone can purify it perfectly but this act of divine grace becomes more effective when the heart is purged of evil thoughts by means of *dhikr* or method of recollection and *murāqabat* i.e. meditation. Hun-

ger, solitude and silence are the chief weapons used to conquer *nafs*. The aspirant has
to traverse through a progressive series of
stations (*maqāmat*) and the highest end is
attained by means of exercises in spiritual
meditation and recollectedness which prepare
the aspirant for ecstatic experience. Ecstasy
here recognizes two aspects of the experience
of oneness with God, symbolized by negative
terms like *fana* (losing individuality), *faqd*
(self-loss), *sukr* (intoxication) and their positive counterparts *baqa* (abiding in God), *wajd*
(finding God) and *sahw* (sobriety). To abide
in God (*baqa*) after having passed away from
selfhood (*fana*) is the mark of the Perfect
man, who not only journeys to God, but in
and with God, he returns with God to the
phenomenal world from which he set out.

Like leaders of other religious traditions
the Sufi leaders too considered meditation
as essential for spiritual growth. Meditation
does not mean philosophical thought or
poetic flight, but something more. It is by
means of meditation that an aspirant is able
to penetrate the very depths of reality. Meditation is a means of concentration which the
aspirant makes use of in order to elevate his

consciousness far above the normal plane. In the beginning human consciousness remains intimately attached to the lower aspects of its individuality. In order to effect separation of these two aspects one should gradually warm up the whole of his psychic being, until it has purged out of the inmost layers of our subconscious all evil thoughts.

Meditation demands uninterrupted flow of the same thought of God. The mind easily succumbs to a thought which it is subjected to uninterruptedly for a long time. The human mind is like a laundered cloth which takes the colour of the dye in which it is dipped. Meditation is well-established concentration of mind and it is a useful source of strength. Swami Vivekananda said, "There is no limit to the power of the human mind. The more concentrated it is, the more power is brought to bear on one point."

To gain control over the *nafs* and for *muraqabat* (meditation) and *muhasab* (self examination) the aspirant follows a struggle called by the sufis al-Jihad al-Akbar (inner struggle). It consists of the following basic stages:

(a) *Muraqabat* (Meditation): It means being

alive to the conviction that God sees man and man sees God. Tradition says "Righteousness consists in worshipping God as if thou seest Him; for if thou seest Him not, yet He sees thee." It creates in the heart an all-impelling reverence for God. It serves to exalt the supreme majesty and glory of God, which practice leads man to his absorption in God.

(b) *Muhasaba* (self-examination): The practicant must take account of his actions at every step and examine them carefully. If he finds himself guilty, he must chastise himself, through punishment, lest it should occur again.

(c) *Fiqr* (Reasoning): Reasoning is the essential condition of *muraqabat*. Its utility is twofold. On the one hand it gives knowledge of self and on the other hand it gives rise to the various stages of the self.

These are followed by *Ikhlas* (sincerity) *Sidq* (truthfulness), *Khauf* and *Raja* (fear and hope), *Tawwakul* (reliance), *Riza* (satisfaction) and *Shukr* (thankfulness). At this stage he believes that God is his well-wisher more than he himself and really knows what is good for him.

The mind is a very changeable entity. A man is serene only when he reaches a condition mentioned above in which he has burned his bridges behind him.

The practice of Sufism is built upon two corner stones: (*a*) Spiritual teacher, *pir, murshid* or *Shaikh* and (*b*) love. *Murshid* is the person who is able to satisfy the seeking impulse of a *talib* (disciple). The love should be voluntary, selfless, abundant, all-encompassing. This love is a way to truth, to knowledge and to action. The initiation into Sufism is considered a second birth or spiritual birth. Suhrawardi recommends a forty days' seclusion for prayer and fasting once a year. Shorn of worldly belongings, the aspirant should pray two *Rakas* in clean dress and sitting on a clean prayer carpet and repent for his past sins with weeping and humility. During his retirment he should regularly perform ablutions; he should sleep only when over-powered by fatigue. He should continue repeating his *dhikr* until he grows weary.

The broad outline of Sufi asceticism as has been dealt by Ghazali comprises an ordinary religious duty of purification, prayers,

almsgiving, fasting and pilgrimage. And to
their aid comes additional acts of devotion
like recitation of Quran, praise of God (*dhikr*)
supplication (*dua*) and vigils.

For attaining spiritual perfection one has
to follow purgative and unitive methods—
the first one purifies the heart by subduing
the passions, while the other leads to union
with God by the acquisition of virtues and
faculties. Before entering on his novitiate
an aspirant must renounce wealth, reputa-
tion, mechanical conformity (*Taqlid*) and sin.
He must then cling to his *Shaikh* who will
provide him with four weapons against the
assault of Satan, *viz.*, solitude, silence, fasting
and sleeplessness. Now begins the long inward
struggle against lusts and passions. When
these are vanquished the aspirant should only
continually repeat some *dhikr* like 'Allah! Allah!
Subhana'llah !" (Glory to God), until the
essential meaning of it fills his heart. Then the
Shaikh may enjoin him to apprehend rightly
the divine reality (*Haqiqat*). He will bid him
to meditate assiduously in order to have illumination. This is a perilous path and the *Shaikh*
has to take great care of his disciple. The weak
should stick to simple faith and practical

devotion. However, all those engaged in devotion have to be aware of pitfalls, like vain glory, hypocrisy, delight in visions and miracles. After this resume of the *purgative way,* Ghazali treats in detail the various passions and vices, from lust and gluttony to the spiritual pride, their nature, symptoms, diagnosis and the effective remedies in each case.

The *unitive way* may be expounded under the heads, (i) repentance, (ii) patience and thanksgiving, (iii) fear and hope, (iv) poverty and renunciation, (v) unification (*tauhid*) and trust in God, (vi) love, desire, intimacy and acquiescence, (vii) intention, sincerity and truth (viii) contemplation (*muraqabat*) and self-examination (*muhasaba*), (ix) reflexion (*tapkkur* and (x) meditation on death and what comes after it.

Al-Qushairi, while analysing the moral and psychological advancement of a mystic, pointed out fortyfive steps. His predecessor Al-Sarraj enumerated seven stations (conversion, abstinence, renunciation, poverty, patience, trust in God and satisfaction) and ten states (meditation, nearness to God, love, fear, hope, longing, intimacy, tranquillity, contemplation and cert-

14

ainty). Here *Maqam* (or station) is a stage of attainment in the pilgrim's progress to God. It results mostly from the mystic's personal endeavour. But *hal* is a spiritual mood gifted by God. The aspirant after winning over his animal soul at one *maqam* steps forward for the next with the help of *hal*.

Though each Order has its own rules they generally agree in the following points for every aspirant: (i) an elaborate ceremony of initiation, which is preceded by a long and arduous apprenticeship; (ii) the wearing of a peculiar habit or costume; (iii) a severe discipline of solitude, prayer, fasting and other austerities; (iv) the immoderate use of *dhikr* with the help of music, dancing, etc., to excite ecstasy; (v) belief in extraordinary 'spiritual powers' vouch-safed to adepts, which they display by chewing live coals, etc., ; and (vi) veneration, approaching to deification of the *Shaikh* or head of the Order.

In spite of general agreement there are striking differences in the methods pursued and recommended by great *murshids*. The aspirant's task is that he shoud break down the different enclosures by which his ego is isolated from the ultimate Totality. He should be careful that he does not reduce or mutilate his existence; on the other hand he should ensure that it is one of continuous growth and of infinite enlargement. Thus he approaches, step by step, towards the ultimate truth. The passions, impulses, greeds and desires are the hidden enemies. Subtle thoughts and desires lie hidden in the human mind, waiting to spring up at the first opportunity. We have to keep a great part of our mind free from the domination of derogatory impulses and desires, so that the mind, thus freed, can think of God. Muhammed Amini's method of meditating the *dhikr* formula *lā ilāha illa'llāh* recommends: Keep the tongue fixed firmly to the roof of the mouth. After drawing a deep breath, you should hold it, and make a beginning with the word *lā*. Imagine that you are taking it from below the navel; let it extend along the organs *qalb*—heart, *rih*—spirit, *sirr*—inmost conscience, *khafi* hidden depth, *akhfā*—most hidden depth, and finally bring it up to the rational soul (*al-nafs al-nātiqa*) which is in the first lobe of the brain. Follow this up by taking the *hamza* of *ilāha*—in imagination—from the brain, then let it descend until it finishes at the right shoulder blades; then draw it down the *ruh* (two fingers' breadth below

the right nipple towards the breast). Now
imagine that you are taking the *hamza* of *illa'
llāh* from the shoulder·blade; let it slide down
the edge of the middle of the breast until it
finishes at the *qalb* (heart, two fingers' breadth
below the nipple towards the side), which may
be imagined at this point as beating to the World
of Majesty, with all the force of the pent-up
breath pressing against the core of the heart,
until its effect and heat are felt throughout
the body. Its heat will burn up all the corrupt
practicles of the body, while the sound particles
will be irradiated by the Light of Majesty.
This process is to be repeated 21 times, not
automatically but reflectively and with due
regard to the meaning of the formula meditated.
At the end of this exertion, the *jhākir* will
experience the result of his *dhikr qalbi*; he will
lose all consciousness of being a man and a part
of creation, and his pettiness will be entirely
destroyed in the attraction of the Divine Essence.

To achieve the perfect view of the Sufis
(*Muraquiba-i-Nizami*), *i.e.,* realisation of multiplicity in unity and unity in multiplicity, the
spiritual aspirant has to contemplate on the
phenomenal existence. He must be convinced
that all things are but shadows or reflections of

the ideas of God or essence of things reflected in the mirror of the existence of God. Next he should contemplate on the Divine by being convinced that God subsists in His own self and possesses His attributes. Without any substantive change He has manifested Himself in the form of phenomenal things through the attributes of Light. Closing his eyes the aspirant should contemplate that his well-known self was not his true self. In fact God has manifested Himself in that form. By meditating on the concept, "I do not exist, God alone exists", he perceives God within. Then contemplating God without he ushers in a state of "self-forgetfulness". The aspirant must devote his life to prayer, contemplation and communion with God, feeling God's intimate presence within and sensing his presence without. When such remembrance continues without break the aspirant enters permanently into the presence of God. The stage is called *Yaddasht*. If God wills, this contemplation may lead to the state declared by the Prophet, "I have sometimes a moment in God which neither the most intimate angels of God nor his Messengers can attain thereto."

A cautious pilgrim is aware that the mind

tricks an aspirant in many different ways. The mind like a spirited horse will try to dislodge the aspirant, but upon finding that he cannot be shaken off, it will become his slave. Once the aspirant makes the determination to ride it and this determination is coupled with concentration of mind he becomes sure of victory. A well-disciplined aspirant easily wins over the *nafs* and advances in his journey from the outward to the inward. An aspirant must become aware of what one has always been from eternity (*azal*), but this is not possible until the entire transformation is brought about in the soul through Divine presence (*hadur*). When the knowledge of divine presence illumines the mind it is filled with the love of God. Together with such perfect gnosis, love and devotion gush up in the mind of the gnostic and in such a state he, though living in the world, enters into Heaven.

—O—

WORSHIP IN ISLAM

MD. ZAINULABEDEEN

1. Meditation, concentration and worship are spiritual exercises that draw man nearer to God and make him dearer to his Creator. In these exercises there is involvement of mind, soul and body. Body is the vehicle of mind, and mind is the mirror which focusses on the divine soul which in its turn guides in spiritual realisation. To hasten this process cleanliness of body to a certain extent, and purity and steadiness of mind to the greatest possible degree are highly essential. Man's living conditions have to be evaluated in the light of the above objective so that the whole human system can be geared to achieve his spiritual goal in a steady systematic manner. Life based on correctly evaluated principles is indeed the successful life. To have what is good in this life, and consequently a good hereafter, are indeed the real objectives of human existence.

2. The Holy Quran teaches an important expression of entreaty to God which is repeated

daily again and again by Muslims. "O Lord!
give unto us in the world that which is good and
in the Hereafter that which is good, and guard
us from the doom of fire." (2:201)

3. Worship is a comprehensive term which
includes all modes of spiritual exercises practised
by the body, mind and soul of an individual or
by a group of persons together. This is generally called prayer in common parlance, and is
used in respect of God. Prayer means experi-
encing the presence of God, strengthening bonds
of attachment, hymning His praise and humbly
expressing gratitude for all the blessings. These
spiritual exercises during certain times of day
and night infuse a deep consciousness of His
beneficent existence, whatever be the other
avocations of our day to day life, with all its
stresses and strains. This experience is aptly
described by Sri Ramakrishna through the
example of a servant maid who works in the
house of her master, deeply involved in all
activities and completely identifying herself with
them all the day round, but still not forgetting
the fact that she has a sweet home of her
own wherein live her children. It all depends
on the intensity of attachment one develops,
and every wave of consciousness of this attach-

ment to the Divine Presence gives one absolute satisfaction and profound peace. "Verily in the remembrance of God do hearts find rest," says the Holy Quran (13:28). To achieve this lasting consciousness is the fulfilment of human experience; and one has to develop this consciousness and guard it as the most precious possession.

4. In Islam, worship of God is an obligatory duty for every Muslim. It should be very clearly understood, that Islam is a pure and unadulterated monotheism. God is one and to Him alone is our prayer or worship due. This is the first article of Muslim faith. There is no compromise on this. He is the Absolute: His sovereignty is not shared by another. So that in Islam, worship of minor deities, saints and other lesser beings amounts to rank apostasy. The Muslim prayer is a direct relationship between man and God and does not recognise any intermediary. God says in the Holy Quran: "Pray unto Me and I will hear your prayer." (40 : 60) "Verily We created man and We know what his soul whispers and We are nearer to him than his jugular vein" (50 : 16).

5. The obligatory prayer in Islam called

salat has been standardised by the Holy Prophet Muhammad under Divine guidance. *Salat*
is the humble supplication of the individual to
his Creator, glorifying Him and seeking His
mercy, protection and guidance. Evil
thoughts and desires are expelled from the
minds of those who regularly offer *salat*. The
Holy Quran says, "Surely, *salat* restrains (one)
from indecent and evil deeds; and the remembrance of God is the greatest (thing in life)
without doubt" (29 : 45). It is a stream
that purifies man every time he takes a dip
in it. It results in closer bonds with the Creator
and develops submission and peace. In fact it
lays the foundations of a real successful life.
The call for prayer from every mosque five
times a day, includes two significant brief
sentences: "Come for *salat*, come for success."

6. *Salat* has to be frequently observed
for it to become a regular feature of daily
life. The wavering mind can thus be trained
to attune itself to constant remembrance of
God. "Establish prayer for My remembrance",
says God in the Holy Quran (20 : 14). Consciousness of God is the controlling force which
guards and guides, and maintains the purity of
action in human thought, word and deed. Thus

human endeavour in any aspect, with this
Divine Consciousness, becomes itself an act
of worship. While engaged in work in such
mental climate, one feels supreme satisfaction
and develops perfect peace. The mode of life
or the type of work is not by itself the criterion.
Tensions, stresses and strains do not come in the
way. Avarice and jealously will be foreign to
the aspirant. Such a life in this world is really
successful and fulfilling and serves as a good
preparation and base for success in the hereafter
too. Therefore, response to the call of *salat*
is indeed the means for realisation of success
in both the worlds.

7. The compulsory standardised *salat* is
fixed at five times a day. The first prayer is
at dawn, when in the calm and peaceful atmosphere God is remembered and glorified. The
day thus begins with a holy consciousness. The
next two prayers are in early and late afternoons,
when in the midst of worldly activities God is
not forgotten. The fourth prayer is just after
sun-set, and the fifth and final for the day is at
any time before midnight, so that the end of the
day's activity is also marked by a prayer. The
mode of offering *salat* is also unique in Islam.
Mind, word and body are simultaneously invol-

ved in the observance of *salat*. It starts with a
steady standing posture facing the Kaba (the
first house of God in Mecca) with arms folded
and with the consciousness of being face to
face with God.

8. "Lo! I have turned my face towards
Him who has created the heavens and the
earth and I am not one of those that associate
others with Divine sovereignty" (Quran 6:79)

9. The first chapter or *surah* of the Holy
Quran containing seven brief sentences is
the most important oft-repeated *surah* in the
standing posture. This is called *Al Fatihah*.
This is followed by any other short *surah*
or part of any other long *surah* from the Holy
Quran. This standing posture is followed by
two other postures indicating extreme humility
namely bowing with palms on knees, and
prostrating on folded legs with forehead touching
the ground, hymning praise and glory of God.
This is followed by sitting for a while in a comfortable position, invoking God's mercy and
peace on the Prophet and his kin and on himself and those connected with him.

10. *Al Fatihah* is universal in its scope
and profound in its content. It is the essence
of the Holy Quran and the heart of Muslim

prayer. The rest of the Qurani chapters are a graphic commentary on Al Fatihah, whose translation reads as follows:—

1. In the name of God, Most Gracious, Most Merciful.

2. Praise is only to God,
   The Cherisher and Sustainer of the worlds,

3. Most Gracious, Most Merciful,

4. Master of the Day of Judgement,

5. Thee (alone) do we worship
   And to Thee (alone) we pray for help.

6. Show us the straight way,

7. The way of those whom thou hast blessed; not (the way) of those who incur Thine wrath, not of those who go astray.

This *surah* can be divided into three distinct parts. It starts with the praise of God, and lays down that He alone deserves praise. This cuts at the root of the tendency in man to praise any other person or object. It mentions the most important attributes of God—Rab, Rahman, Rahim, and Malik. It is difficult to translate these words; but they indicate His Sovereignty, abiding Grace and

15

limitless Mercy (1 to 4). In the second part
(item 5) man's relationship is firmly established
with that Almighty alone, elevating man to the
status of his direct devotee, and affirming the
supreme and undivided sovereignty of God.
In the third part man beseeches God to guide
him along the correct and straight path which
leads to success in this and the next worlds.
The sequence in the presentation of *Al Fatihah*
shows that it is a petition or address to the
Almighty submitted by the whole humanity
without distiction of caste or community.

11. In addition to the compulsory, sub-
sidiary or optional *salat,* it can also be offered
during other parts of the day and the night
depending on one's convenience. The Holy
Quran recommends offering of optional prayer
in the small hours of the night. This is called
"*tahajjud*". Some Muslims regularly observe
this in addition to the five compulsory prayers.
Salat can be observed in any clean place treating
the whole universe as the temple of God. It
can be done individually or in congregation in
the nearest mosque. Joining in the congrega-
tional prayers is highly recommended, because
it develops brotherhood and fellow-feeling.

12. In effect the Qurani teachings and
its revelations lead to an understanding of

the working of the universe and the universal Power behind. Says God in the Holy Quran: "Lo! in the creation of the heavens and the earth and (in) the alternation of night and day are signs (of His sovereignty) for men of understanding. Such (men) remember God standing, sitting and reclining, and consider the creation of the heavens and the earth, and say "O Lord! Thou did not create this in vain; Glory be to Thee;save us from the doom of fire"(3:190,191).

It should however be understood that this exercise, however intense, does not absolve any Muslim from offering the compulsory *salat*.

13. Another important feature of Muslim worship has also to be emphasised. Mere belief in God's unity and sovereignty, followed however regularly by obligatory prayers, does not by itself lead to spiritual fulfilment. Faith and worship must be followed by righteous conduct. Otherwise this exercise is in vain. The Holy Quran is very clear on this. It says, 'Lo! the noblest of you, in the sight of God, are those best in conduct". (49 : 13).

What is righteous conduct is detailed in the chapters of the Holy Quran. Thus, Muslim worship consists not only of *salat* but also of good conduct following it.

SADHANA IN SRI MADHVA'S PHILOSOPHY

Dr. P. NAGARAJA RAO

The Philosophy of Sri Madhva is not merely a theory of reality working out a well-rounded system satisfying the intellectual's instinct for consistency and non-contradiction. It is that and something more. It is a way of life for the attainment of *mokṣa*, which state of existence puts not only an end to the threefold suffering man is heir to but also secures him eternal bliss. To secure this, man has to follow a way of life adumbrated by the triple texts. The way is called the Sadhana.

Sadhana is a complex term which blends all the resources of man for the attainment of *mokṣa*. One obtains the knowledge of philosophical truths through reverent study of the scriptures with devotion under the guidance of a competent Guru. Going to the Guru is not an act of formality. It is a spiritual necessity. For the Guru knows the path as he has trodden it. It is called *śravaṇa*. Self-study is not *śravaṇa*.

What is taught by the Guru must be thought out in a dialectical way by the Sadhaka examining its pros and cons until the scripture-taught doctrines become his settled conviction. This is called *manana.* Intellectual examination supported by scripture has a place, though limited, in the philosophy of Madhva. Any belief is not philosophy. Examined belief is philosophy. After *manana,* the Sadhaka contemplates the Lord until such time as he has His direct vision called *aparokṣajnāna.* God-vision enables the Sadhaka to love the Lord intensely because he knows the Lord first hand. He practises *parā bhakti.* This results in the grace of the Lord, *prasāda*, which removes the bondage of the soul, which is real. The removal of the bondage makes the soul realize his own true nature, *svasvarūpatā.* Such a realization is called *mokṣa.* *Mokṣa* is through grace and not through mere self-effort, which is necessary but not sufficient.

In all the stages of spiritual *sādhana,* right from the *śravaṇa* stage, Bhakti is necessary.

Śravaṇaṁ mananaṁ caiva dhyānaṁ bhak-
tistathaiva ca
Sādhanaṁ jñānasampattau pradhānaṁ
nānyadiṣyate

Bhaktyā jñānaṁ tato bhaktiḥ tato dṛṣṭis-
tataśca sā-
Tato muktistato bhaktiḥ saiva syāt sukha
rūpiṇī:

From Bhakti arises Jnana, from that arises
further Bhakti, from that the vision of God.
Vision strengthens further *parā bhakti*. That
releases the soul, and the state of release and
devotion to Lord consitutes bliss. In short Sri
Madhva's philosophy is a *bhakti-siddhānta*.
Release is obtained only through the grace of
the Lord and without it there is no hope for it.

Nārāyaṇa prasādamṛte na mokṣaḥ

If it is so, what should the individual do?
Should he sit with folded hands or practise
intense *sādhana* to obtain the grace of the Lord?
Sri Madhva asks the simple question: what
should man do after learning the scriptures and
understanding their chief import?

Samanvayāvirodhābhyāṁ   samjāte vastu-
nirṇaye
Kim mayā kāryamityeva syād buddhi-
radhikāriṇaḥ

Man, being not an insentient object, has
to practise a course of *sādhana,* which goes into
two types—scriptural study and contemplation.

Sopāsanā caidvividhā śāstrābhyāsasvarū-
piṇī
Dhyānarūpā parā caiva tadaṅgaṁ dhāraṇ-
ādikam

Sri Madhva believes that scriptural study requires more concentration than contemplation. So he is all praise for it. The *sādhaka* undertakes *upāsanā*, worship of the Lord, suited to his svarūpa and worships the Lord according to his eligibility. In the eloquent words of Jayatirtha—"The Lord is unmanifest by His nature. Without the aid of His grace it is not possible to have His vision in spite of a thousand human efforts. Lo! When His grace visits us we have His direct vision by His powers."

The means for His immediate vision is His grace and blessing. This cannot be had except by worshipful devotion to the Lord who is free of all defects and is full of auspicious attributes. The devotion must be continuous and constant with detachment towards objects and practised for a long time. This is called Nididhyāsana.

Na ca avyaktasvabhāvo bhagavān sahas-
renāpi prayatnena śakyaḥ sākṣatkartum
vinā tadanugrahāt.

Prasannastu ananyacintyayogāt ātmānaṁ
                              darśayāti iti yujyate

Darśanasādhanaṁ cānugrahaḥ. Svayog-
    yaguṇopetasya nirdoṣasya bhagavadvi-
    grahaviśeṣasya ādaranairantaryābhyām
    viṣayavairāgyabhaktisahitāt bahukalo-
    pacitāt nididhyāsanāparanāmakāt vici-
                   nvatāt ṛte na labhyate.

The devotee must not sit with folded arms,
waiting for the Lord to do everything. He
must roll up the sleeves and go to work.
Though the Lord does not need man's work,
yet His resolve in the governance of the world
is that men should make some effort and ask
the Lord for refuge.

Sarvajno'pi hi viśveśaḥ sadā kāruṇiko'pi
                                          san
Samsāratantravāhitvāt rakṣāpekṣām pratī-
                                        kṣate.

Sādhana, Jayatirtha observes, is of two
types—that which is there already (siddha)
and that which has to be attained (sādhya)
The Lord is the *siddha sādhana*. Man, by
his effort and devotion has to activate the grace
of the Lord as the wood cutter splits the wood
with the axe and the sacrificer derives the fruit
by the sacrifice.

Sādhanam ca dvividham, siddhamasid-
dham ca.

Tatra asiddham utpādyam phalakāmena,
yatha yāgād

Siddham tu savyāpārīkaraṇīyam, yatha-
kuṭhārādi.

Siddham ca sādhana bhagavān iti
mumukṣuṇā savyāpārīkaraṇīyaḥ.

Having all this in mind. Sri Madhva
ascribes a certain limited sense of agency to
man (Jivo'pi kartā). After God-vision the
individual soul becomes directly aware of
the glory of the Lord and practises supreme
'devotion', which is a steady continuous
flow of deep attachment to the Lord, unsur-
mountable by any kind of impediment and
a love that transcends love of self, love of
kith and kin, and love of cherished belongings. He must also be fortified and inspired
by the firm conviction of the transcendent
majesty of God as the abode of all perfec-
tions and free from all blemishes. Such a
devotion invokes the grace of the Lord and
removes man's bondage and makes him realize
his own svarūpa, which is mokṣa.

Parameśvara bhaktirnāma niravadhi-kānan-
tānavadhyakalyāṇa guṇatvatānupūrvakaḥ, svā-

tmātmīyasamastavastubhyo 'nekaguṇādhikaḥ,
antarāyasahasreṇāpi apratibaddho nirantara-
premapravāhaḥ. Na casau tat sākṣatkāram anta-
reṇa nipadyate. Loke tathā darsanāt.

The aspirant leads a life of ceremonial
purity, which he keeps or cannot keep when he
is lost in contemplation, with ethical excellence
and constant devotion. Through the grace of
the Lord earned through the *sādhana* of bhakti
he attains mokṣa.

> Ajñānāṁ jñānado viṣṇuḥ
> jñāninām mokṣadaśca saḥ
> Ānandadaścamuktānam
> sa evaiko janārdanaḥ.

ABOUT THE CONTRIBUTORS

1. Swami Siddhinathananda, a senior monk of the Ramakrishna Order is the Head of Ramakrishna Mission Sevashrama, Calicut. He is a prolific writer in both English and Malayalam and has a number of philosophical works to his credit.

2. Swami Ananyananda is the President of the Advaita Ashrama, Mayavati, Himalayas. He has specialised in the writings of Swami Vivekananda.

3. Swami Harshananda, a Senior Monk of the Ramakrishna Order is a good Sanskritist and has published books on Yoga, Temples etc.

4. Prof. B. Kuppuswamy was an outstanding psychologist, who tried to correlate Eastern psychology with the Western.

5. Dr. T. M. P. Mahadevan, Director of the Centre for Advanced Studies of Philosophy, Madras University, was a lucid writer on Advaita and has a number of philosophical treatises to his credit.

6. Swami Vijnananda is the Secretary of Ramakrishna Mission Ashrama, Salem.

7. Swami Nityabodhananda is in charge of Ramakrishna Vivekananda Centre at Geneva. He was a former editor of the Vedanta Kesari and is a fluent writer and speaker in English and French.

8. Swami Paratparananda is in charge of the Ramakrishna Ashrama, Buenos Aires, Argentina. He has published works in Spanish on Ramakrishna-Vivekananda literature.

9. Swami Sastrananda, a Senior Monk of the Ramakrishna Order, is a very impressive speaker and writer.

10. Dr. Anima Sen Gupta is the Retired Head of the Dept. of Philosophy of Patna University. She is a regular contributor on Sankhya and other philosophical systems to many journals.

11. Dr. Sampooran Singh, Retd. Director, Defence Laboratory, has made a comparative study of Spirituality and Science.

12. Dr. B.S. Surti is a Retired member of the Andhra Medical Service and is a specialist in Zorastrianism. He has compiled the *Thus Spake Zarathushtra* published by the Sri Ramakrishna Math, Madras, in the *Thus Spake* series.

13. Swami Prabhananda is a Trustee of the Ramakrishna Math and a member of the Governing Body of the Ramakrishna Mission. He has made a deep study of Sufi literature.

14. Janab Md. Zainulabedeen is a Retired officer of the Andhra Agricultural Service.

15. Dr. P. Nagaraja Rao has taught philosophy in many universities in India and was also for a time 'Swami Vivekananda Professor of Comparative Philosophy,' in the University of Madras.